"You can try to shape an oak tree when it is twenty to thirty years old, or more. But you are likely to spend hours and fortunes with little to show for your effort. Gregg is a master at shaping lives of young men and women when they are still saplings and haven't set down their tap root. He gives them the start they need to reach high and branch wide with their messages of the love of God."

–PETER HERSCHEND, co-founder and co-owner
of Herschend Family Entertainment (formerly
Silver Dollar City, Inc.), former president of the
Missouri State Board of Education

"Many biographies tell about the accumulation of wealth or title. Gregg's biography tells a different story of passion to serve God.

"I recommend that my friends read Gregg's story because it offers the path to a well-lived life. It's my hope that as you read these pages, you, too, will feel a solid nudge to trust God with your life."

–JACK HERSCHEND, co-founder and chairman
emeritus of Herschend Family Entertainment

I0542012

ADVANCE PRAISE

"Gregg is a full living example of God's beautiful economy—that nothing ever goes to waste and setbacks are just new opportunities seeking a redemptive outcome."

–TOM RITCHEY, American bicycle frame builder,
Category 1 racer, fabricator, designer, and founder
of Ritchey Design

"I've known Gregg for decades. When I first met him (and Janell), my first impression was not his sense of adventure, but his sense of friendship. He has an extraordinarily strong love for God and people. God uses him in extraordinary ways, as you can tell by reading his story.

"Maybe he can't see how brightly his light shines, but it does. And if I were to tell Gregg that, he'd be humble and shift the attention to God, because he really is that enthralled with God. I hope you'll be incredibly moved by this book, or as Gregg would say, by God himself, the source of all he is. And Gregg would be quick to add that that source is available to you, too. To all of us."

–DEBBIE JOHNSON, author, blogger, pianist,
founder/director of DenverWorks, and executive
director of India Transformed

"When I grow up, I want to be just like Gregg Bettis. He loves Jesus, his family, friends, and adventure. This book chronicles a life well lived in faithful service to Christ. Gregg challenges all of us to take risks and trust God. Do yourself a favor and read this book slowly. You'll be glad you did."

–TED CUNNINGHAM, senior pastor of Woodland
Hills Family Church, author of *Fun Loving You*

"Gregg has lived an adventurous life that most of us only dream about. By God's grace, he lived to share his adventures in this book. Hold your breath and open your heart as you read about God's faithfulness through it all."

–KEN DAVIS, Christian comedian, speaker, author, and president of Dynamic Communications International

"One of the greatest misnomers about the God of the Universe is that life with Christ is simply a list of do's and don'ts. For many years, I believed that following God meant that I had to stop doing everything that was awesome in life. Fortunately, God, in His divine authorship, placed men and women in my life to show me otherwise. Gregg Bettis is one of those men. Gregg has shown me what it looks like to go on an adventure with God. His book, *Crashes and Climbs*, will influence you the same way Gregg has influenced me. Your faith will swell with each turn of the page and you will be inspired to join the adventure!"

–SHAY ROBBINS, podcast host, author, financial advisor for Robbins Financial, and chief strategy officer for the Robbins Group

"Entertaining. Enlightening. Encouraging. Inspiring.

"Life is about climbing, slipping, falling, finding our footing, and seizing opportunities to reach out and up to our faithful God... and to discover the beauty and majesty of our creator. Gregg has always chosen to learn and grow from his setbacks, failures, and falls. He has chosen to faithfully practice what he has taught. God has used his faithfulness and trust in Him and his love of adventure to meaningfully impact countless lives. This is one of those unique books that you'll want to share with your friends."

–GARY J. OLIVER, THM, PHD, licensed clinical psychologist, professor emeritus of psychology & practical theology at John Brown University, and author of over twenty books

CRASHES
&CLIMBS

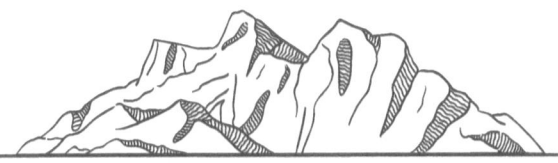

CRASHES
&CLIMBS

STORIES FROM A LIFE
LIVED ON THE EDGE

GREGG BETTIS

CRASHES AND CLIMBS
Stories from a Life Lived on the Edge

Copyright © 2024 by Gregg Bettis

Disclaimer: Although the publisher and the author have made every effort to ensure that the information in this book was correct at press time and while this publication is designed to provide accurate information in regard to the subject matter covered, the publisher and the author assume no responsibility for errors, inaccuracies, omissions, or any other inconsistencies herein and hereby disclaim any liability to any party for any loss, damage, or disruption caused by errors or omissions, whether such errors or omissions result from negligence, accident, or any other cause.

All Scripture quotations, unless otherwise indicated, are taken from the Holy Bible, New International Version®, NIV®. Copyright ©1973, 1978, 1984, 2011 by Biblica, Inc.™ Used by permission of Zondervan. All rights reserved worldwide. www.zondervan. com. The "NIV" and "New International Version" are trademarks registered in the United States Patent and Trademark Office by Biblica, Inc.™

Scripture quotations marked (NASB) are taken from the (NASB®) New American Standard Bible®, Copyright © 1960, 1971, 1977, 1995, 2020 by The Lockman Foundation. Used by permission. All rights reserved. lockman.org

Interior Layout and Design by Stephanie Anderson
Book Cover Design by Abigael Elliott

ISBN:
979-8-89165-095-4 *Paperback*
979-8-89165-096-1 *Hardback*
979-8-89165-097-8 *E-book*

Published by:
Streamline Books
Kansas City, MO
streamlinebookspublishing.com

CONTENTS

This book is dedicated to my bride, Janell Bettis, who has lovingly stood by my side all these years and exuberantly loved Jesus, life, her family, and nature; to our daughter Kaylene, her husband Bryan, and our "wonderful one" granddaughter Amy Grace Gerard, who always brightens up my day and makes me smile; to my amazing parents, who have continued to love me regardless of my crazy, adventurous lifestyle; and to all who have helped me climb the mountains within and cheered me on in my wild-at-heart journey through life and in writing this book. I love you all.

"To venture is to risk one's life, but not to venture is to lose one's life."

–Unknown

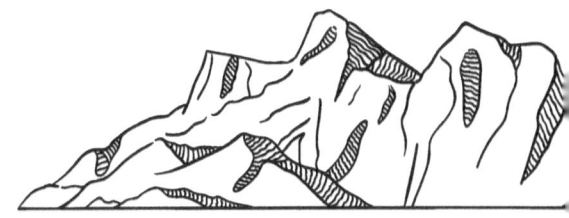

INTRODUCTION

MY LIFE HAS always been either a daring,
exciting adventure or nothing. As a wild little
boy, I dreamed of conquering the four-thou-
sand-foot mountain I could see out my bedroom window,
and that same spirit still lives inside me today. I've never
known the definition of the word "relax," and I've always
said that if I'm not living on the edge, I'm probably taking
up too much space. It's never been my intention to arrive
at my own grave with a handsome, well-preserved body,
but rather to slide into it sideways in a cloud of dust, totally
used up, completely worn out, and loudly shouting, "Wow!
What an incredible ride!"

I've experienced so many amazing things in my life that
there's sadly not room for them all in this book. I've stared
death in the face more times than I can count—plane crashes, risky technical climbs, close encounters with bears. I've
seen demons cast out and lives turned around. I've seen God

change hearts and save people by His amazing power and grace (including me).

But what I'm sharing here isn't about me. It's all about God—how He's guided me, led me into amazing adventures, and preserved and protected me through it all, from the day I was born until now. This book is me, prayerfully sharing God's story for my life in hopes that it might be an encouraging catalyst to anyone who reads it. My hope is that my story would inspire you to use your time, talent, and treasure to build God's kingdom, and that it would encourage you that even now, God is present, alive, and showing up in powerful ways.

Since the day I encountered Jesus in my own Damascus Road experience (which I'll share more about later in this book), I've sensed what I call "sacred echoes" almost daily, calling me to step out by faith in obedience—to follow God into a life of adventure even though I may not understand where I am going or why He might be leading me there. Sometimes this might just be a matter of making a phone call or going to visit someone, but other times it's something big, ominous, and far outside even my own very wide comfort zone.

I've always related strongly with God's call in Genesis 12:1: "The Lord had said to Abram, 'Go from your country, your people and your father's household to the land I will show you.'" There have been many times when I've sensed Him saying to me, "Gregg, I want you to go—to leave everyone and everything you know and go on an adventure with me."

And every time I've acted on that call, God has been so incredibly faithful.

One thing I've always tried to remember is that when I'm entering uncharted waters, God isn't just going with me—He's already there. He's been there preparing the work that He has for me to do, and when He calls me, He never leaves my side. I'm not alone, and as long as I'm willing to follow Him, He'll guide my steps. Like Proverbs 3:5-6 says, "Trust in the Lord with all your heart and lean not on your own understanding; in all your ways submit to him, and he will make your paths straight."

That's what He's done for me. I've leaned on Him, not on myself, and at the most critical times, He's always shown up for me. He's paired me with others who have come alongside me when I've gone into uncharted territory. He's always been faithful to protect me, preserve me, and provide exactly what I need.

As a son of the living God, I have had the privilege of experiencing some amazing opportunities in my life. Through everything God's done for me, I've been able to see His goodness, faithfulness, and amazing love in some incredible ways. I share my life story not because I think there is anything particularly special about it, but because I want you to understand how great and capable God is of using anyone's life to accomplish His goals. My hope is that my story would encourage you in your own adventure with God—that it would embolden you to step out and follow Him wherever He's called you, even if it's somewhere beyond your comfort zone, knowing that no matter where you're going, He's already there.

I pray that God would use this book in your life to guide you exactly where He wants you to go. Thank you for coming on this adventure with me.

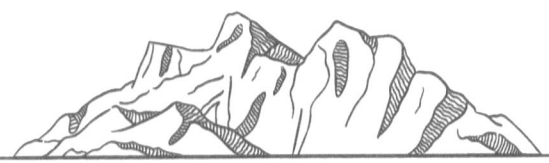

PART ONE

Called to Adventure

> *"The place where God calls you is the place where your deep gladness and the world's deep hunger meet."*
>
> —FREDERICK BUECHNER

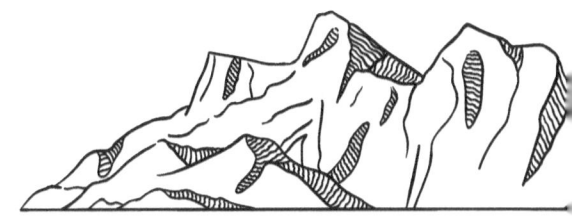

CHAPTER 1

Life Preservers

> *"You live and you learn…*
> *only if you live."*
>
> –UNKNOWN

NOTHING FELT DIFFERENT to me about that Friday night. It was sophomore year, I had just left a high school football game with four of my friends, and we were hanging out at Emmett's Pizza Parlor. We were talking, laughing, and reminiscing about the game, the day, and all the dumb things we were probably about to do over the weekend.

We finished our pizza, but we weren't ready for the night to end. So, we went out to get some beer. None of us were old enough, but we knew where to get it. We drove to an orchard party on the outskirts of town where we wouldn't get caught drinking, and pretty soon the beer was gone.

My buddies wanted to get more, and one of them had the idea to go visit some girls he knew who lived nearby in Concord, California. I had to work the next morning, though, so I told them I couldn't go. I wasn't excited about hitchhiking home by myself, so I told my friend Jimmy that he wasn't going either—he was coming with me. Jimmy wasn't happy about it, but he finally agreed.

As our friends drove away toward Concord with a fresh case of beer, Jimmy and I started hitchhiking toward home. After a while, a car slowed down and pulled up next to us. The driver said he could take us where we were going, so we hopped in. And what happened next will be seared into my memory for the rest of my life.

The guy was listening to KEWB Channel 91 on the radio, and they were playing a Moody Blues song, "Tuesday Afternoon." But then the song was interrupted by an announcement:

> *"Police are requesting assistance identifying three bodies found after a yellow 1955 Studebaker station wagon crashed while heading northbound on San Miguel Road. Anyone with information, please contact the police department as soon as possible. All drivers on San Miguel Road will please proceed with caution."*

Jimmy and I looked at each other. We didn't say anything. We didn't have to. We knew right away that there was only one 1955 Studebaker station wagon heading north on San Miguel

Road that night. It was heading north toward Concord, bringing a case of beer to a girl's house, along with our three friends whose lives had ended before they ever had the chance to get started.

———

GROWING UP, I believed that God existed, but I never really did anything about it. My mother went to a Lutheran church, so you could say I was raised Lutheran, but that wouldn't really be true. I was confirmed there, but I didn't go to church much during my confirmation period. I think I might have lit the candles once, but that was about it. Any idea of a relationship with God was far from my mind. I had other things to focus on: skiing, cars, and spending as much time as possible in the mountains.

I lucked my way into two great jobs that, combined, paid five times what most of my classmates were making, and the income allowed me to spend money on the things I wanted. I built a Corvette from the ground up. I had a motorcycle and a Jeep. I had the latest and greatest ski equipment. And those were the things I poured my time and energy into. I was obsessed with speed—driving fast cars, skiing fast on the water or down a mountain, even flying with friends in fast planes, which happened to align with my dream career of being a pilot for the US Forest Service.

My life was just about everything a kid like me could have dreamed up. I was always able to earn the money I needed to pursue the things I wanted. I had parents who loved me, and they not only supported my hobbies and passions—they made it possible for the golden days of my childhood to be some of the most cherished memories of my life. We built multiple mountain cabins as I was growing up, and I spent a lot of weekends with my parents in the mountains at one of those cabins. I thought I had the world by the tail, and it didn't feel like my life had much room or much need for Jesus.

But I'll tell you one thing—I may not have been paying attention to Jesus, but He was paying attention to me. All I cared about was becoming a pilot, finding girls I could impress with my Corvette, skiing as much as possible, and racing through mountain roads and trails on my motorcycle. But Jesus had something else in store for me. He had plans to use me in ways I never would have dreamed of, to bless me with opportunities to make an impact on people that would last for eternity. Long before I ever gave Him the time of day, He was preparing and preserving me for that future.

I very easily could have been in that yellow '55 Studebaker station wagon with my friends that night. When they wanted to drive to Concord, I didn't tell them I couldn't come because we'd all been drinking and it wasn't safe. I just wanted to get some sleep before work the next day.

After we heard the announcement on the radio, Jimmy and I convinced the driver who had picked us up to turn around and take us back to the scene of the accident. The sight was unbelievable. The station wagon we'd been riding in less than half an hour ago had crumpled in on itself like it was made of paper. Our friends had missed a corner in the dark, they had run the car straight into a boulder, and all three of them had been ejected through the windshield. Jimmy and I told the police that we knew who the three bodies belonged to. I'll never forget that night for the rest of my life.

I don't know why God allowed me to survive. There's nothing special about me that would suggest I deserve to still be sitting here, writing these words, while my three friends lost their lives far too soon. But what I can say is this: God was faithful to me long before I ever considered being faithful to Him. He had a plan for me, and He wasn't ready to bring me home yet.

I look back and see evidence of God's faithfulness, His goodness, and His protection long before I ever came to know Him personally. I'll share many stories throughout this book of times when I saw God show up, but there are so many more stories that this book doesn't have room to hold, and many of them happened before I ever committed my life to Jesus.

I could tell you about a time when I was just fourteen years old, hitchhiking with a friend, and we were picked up by a complete maniac who started driving in a direction that was not where we asked him to go. He wouldn't let us out of the car when we asked him to stop. I don't know what would have happened if I hadn't broken an empty whiskey bottle over his head so we could escape.

I could tell you about the time I took a Corvette out for a test drive with a friend after we had replaced its cracked frame and both front spindles, driving over a hundred miles per hour until we finally slowed down to about twenty-five to turn the corner back toward my house, only for the new front right spindle to break off and the wheel to tear through the fiberglass all the way back to the door—a break that would have killed both of us if it had happened just thirty seconds earlier.

I could tell you about the time it snowed four or five feet one night when I was skiing with some buddies at Bear Valley, weighing down the trees so much that one huge ponderosa pine fell through the wall at two in the morning right next to where I was sleeping, just feet away from landing on me in my bed and ending my life.

But what I will tell you now—and many more times throughout this book—is that God knew what He wanted to use me for long before I ever opened myself up to Him. He's been protecting me, preparing me, and pursuing me with evidence of His presence for my entire life.

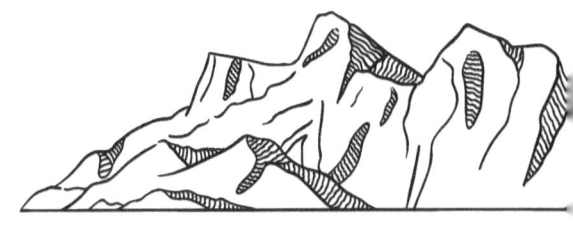

CHAPTER 2

Found By Jesus

> *"The glory of God is*
> *man fully alive!"*
> —IRENAEUS

AFTER I GRADUATED from high school (with a 4.0 GPA, I liked to say—one point for each year) I moved up to the mountains in Sonora, California, to go to Columbia College and pursue my goal of flying for the US Forest Service. I also dreamed of being a semi-professional skier, so living close to the mountains gave me the perfect place to pursue that too. All I wanted to do was fly, ski, and drive fast cars, and I was perfectly positioned to do all three.

Shortly after I moved up to Sonora, my cousin Debbie did too. I was very close to Debbie growing up, and she was like me in a lot of ways—she wasn't interested in church or God or talking to any of those crazy Jesus people. She just wanted to have a good time and enjoy life.

But then she met Steve.

Steve was a youth pastor. He and Debbie started dating, and before long, she could see from Steve's life that there was more to this Jesus stuff than just sitting in an uncomfortable church pew once a week. Steve was different. He had a genuine relationship with Jesus, and it made an impact on her. I won't tell her story here—it's hers to tell—but one way or another, Steve led Debbie to Jesus, and her life changed in a big way.

Of course, none of this mattered much to me. I was still interested in flying, skiing, living life, and doing the things I loved. But as soon as Debbie met Jesus, she decided that I needed to meet Him too. She made it her mission in life to make sure I knew just how much Jesus loved me. She called me often, left me notes, and invited me to come to Sunday evening church with her and Steve every single week. Every Sunday for eighteen months she knocked on my door or called me on the phone, asking me to come to church with her. And every Sunday for eighteen months, I blew her off. I was happy for her, but I made it clear that I didn't want anything to do with church.

None of that stopped Debbie though. And to this day, I thank God that it didn't. She no doubt had everyone in that church praying for me through all eighteen of those months. She didn't quit. She kept coming, Sunday after Sunday. And I was almost as persistent at refusing as she was at inviting.

Almost.

One Sunday afternoon during my freshman year of college, Debbie asked me to come to church. I said no and thought that was the end of it. But a little while later, I heard a knock at my door. It was Debbie again, and she was on her knees, puddles in her eyes. This time, she wasn't just asking—she was begging.

I didn't know what to do. I tried making my normal excuses, but they all sounded particularly feeble on that afternoon. "Debbie," I said, "I just really don't want to go. I'll feel like a total duck out of water. Church is great for you, and I'm happy that it makes you happy. But it just isn't for me."

Debbie looked me in the eye. "If you come with me tonight," she said, "I'll leave you alone for the next two weeks."

I was out of excuses. And it did sound nice to have two weeks of peace. "Fine," I said. "I'll go. But just know that I'm not excited about it. And I want to sit in the back of the church, so nobody stares at me."

Debbie smiled. I didn't know it, and I'm sure she probably didn't either, but her persistence that afternoon was about to change my life forever.

After arriving at Chapel in the Pines and being greeted by a bevy of people, young and old, I made a beeline for the back row. Debbie walked with me, and she guided me to a spot in the back corner. It was in the back, just like I'd asked for, but I think Debbie's true reason for choosing that spot was to keep me from bolting out of the church at my first opportunity.

There were probably a hundred or so college kids in the chapel service, and even from my seat in the back corner, I felt like they could all see right through me. I didn't know any of their songs. I didn't know what to do when they prayed.

Steve gave a message that was probably moving and dynamic, but it all swept right over my head. And I was just sure they could all tell that I didn't belong.

Finally—FINALLY—the service ended. I wanted nothing more than to get out of that church as fast as I could. But as I started making my way toward the door, Debbie grabbed my arm. "Before you leave," she said firmly, "we're going to pray for you."

Great. As if I didn't already feel out of place, now I had to try to stand as non-awkwardly as possible while being prayed for in a place I couldn't wait to get away from. The only thing I wanted to pray for at that moment was that it would all just be over. But I could tell Debbie wasn't going to back down.

"Fine," I told her. "Whatever. Let's get it over with."

Steve joined us, and together, he and Debbie led me back to a small, dimly lit room. It felt a little weird to me, but I didn't have much time to think about it, because as soon as we got to the room, they started praying. "Father, we bind Satan in the name of Jesus. Open Gregg's eyes and ears to hear the truth. Soften his heart. God, reveal yourself to him."

They went on and on like this for what was probably five minutes, but it felt more like an hour. None of the words they were saying meant much to me, but I could tell that if nothing else, they really meant the words they were saying. And it didn't seem like they planned on stopping anytime soon.

So, I decided I'd give God a chance. I wasn't totally sure how to pray, but inside my heart I said to Him, "Okay, God. If you're out there, this is your moment. Reveal yourself. Say something, do something, show me you're out there. Make the lights flicker, shake the building, send thunder and lightning. Just show me you're real, if you're real."

In the next moment, as clearly as if He were standing there in the room with me, I heard God's voice—not audibly, but with deep clarity in my soul. "Gregg, if you don't turn your life over to me tonight," the voice said, "I'm going to wipe you off the face of the planet."

The whole world came screeching to a halt. Everything I had ever thought about God, all the ways I'd tried to run from Him, all the years I'd spent ignoring Him—none of it mattered in that moment. When I heard God tell me what He was going to do if I didn't surrender to Him, all I could think about was how many times my life could have ended already. That night with my friends. The tree falling through the room. All the other near-death experiences I'd already had in my life. To me, the words I heard weren't a threat. They were a reminder of how many times God had already preserved my life—how He'd always been watching out for me, even though I'd been ignoring Him.

I was overwhelmed in that moment with a peace I'd never sensed before. In that moment, I knew beyond any doubt that God was real. And so I replied to Him, inside my heart, "Okay."

Then I said it again, out loud, so Debbie and Steve could hear me. "Okay," I said, "I'll let Jesus be my Savior."

Debbie looked at me, and I expected her to cry or laugh or give me a big hug. Instead, she jabbed her finger into my chest and stared me straight in the eye. "He doesn't want to just be your savior, Gregg," she said. "He wants to be Lord of your life—your pilot in command. He wants complete control of every part of you, from this day forward."

I stared at her, still a little bit in shock. I couldn't believe what was happening. But there was no doubt in my mind—it was happening, and it was real. "Okay," I said. "Okay, Debbie."

And then Debbie's tough exterior broke. She looked at me and began to weep, all her prayer and determination to get me to church over the last eighteen months being released as the tears ran down her cheeks. Steve looked at me, smiling. "Gregg, that's amazing. Would you be willing to follow me in a sinner's prayer—to ask God to forgive your sins and take control of your life?" And right there, on October 2, 1972, I did.

A recent picture of Debbie and me.

It was the first moment in my life I had truly experienced something spiritual. If I'm honest, it's probably the first time I'd ever really opened myself up to it. Looking back, I wonder about the tension I felt walking into that beautiful little Chapel in the Pines church, how I wanted to be just about anywhere else in the world, and I wonder what demonic forces may have been oppressing me. But on that day, I sensed God's power for the first time, and there was no doubt in my mind that it was stronger than Satan's power. Debbie and Steve knew that, and they were praying for God to come meet me before I felt anywhere close to being ready to meet Him.

When I prayed that prayer with Steve, I felt like a huge weight lifted off my shoulders. I began to experience God's amazing presence, power, peace, provision, providence, grace, and mercy for the very first time in my life.

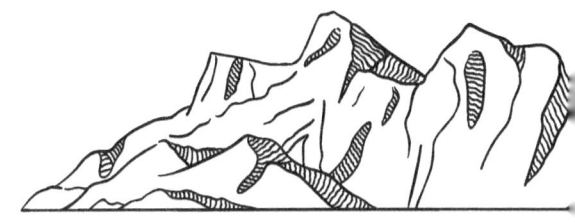

CHAPTER 3

Steve

> *"Life is made of good friends*
> *and great adventures."*
>
> –UNKNOWN

I FELT EXHAUSTED WHEN I finally got home that night, so I went straight to bed. But I couldn't sleep. Too many thoughts raced through my mind too many feelings that I'd never felt before in my life. I was more tired than I'd been in a long time, but somehow, I felt more awake and alive than I ever had.

So, I got up. I walked around my house, looking for anything that I determined wouldn't be helpful to my new life. Over the next two nights, I tore posters off my walls, threw out albums that I felt were not honoring to God, flushed drugs down the toilet, poured out cans of beer and bottles of hard liquor, and disposed of everything else from my house that I thought would be oppressive and could keep me from experiencing the new life I wanted in Jesus.

Then, a couple days later, I finally got up the courage to do something I knew I had to do: I called my best friend Steve.

Steve and I had known each other since junior high, and we'd stayed close even after I left for the mountains to study forestry and fire science at Columbia College. We took turns visiting each other on weekends, and this upcoming weekend it was Steve's turn to come up and visit me. I knew he probably wouldn't be happy to hear about this new change in my life. But I also knew that I had to tell him—not just because I knew I wouldn't be able to hide it from him, but because I wanted him to experience the same powerful peace and presence that I felt in my life now.

So, I picked up the phone and called him. "Hello?" came Steve's voice from the other end.

Two-thousand-mile, classic-convertible road trip with close friend Steve Gustafson.

"Hey, Steve," I said. "What time are you going to be here Friday night? We need to talk."

"I don't know," he said. "Why? What's up?"

"Well," I said, taking a breath, "this past Sunday night, I gave my life to Jesus."

Steve came unglued. "Great," he sneered. "Your cousin finally got to you. Well, you can keep it to yourself. I don't want to hear about any of that craziness. And I won't be coming up at all this weekend."

"No," I said. "You have to listen and trust me, man. Jesus is real. God is real, and He loves us. We have to talk about it."

"I don't want to talk about it," he said. "I'm not coming. I just bought a new bong, and I've got better things to do than listen to you talk about your new church friends."

"Well, if you're not here by ten on Friday, I'm coming to you," I said. "And we're going to talk."

"I'm not coming, and we're not talking," he said. "See ya, Gregg." And he hung up.

Friday arrived, and I wasn't surprised at all to see that Steve was good to his word: he didn't show up. So, I stayed good to my word too. I jumped in my '62 'Vette and made the two-hour drive down to the Bay Area straight to Steve's parents' house, where he still lived, and knocked on the door.

Steve's mom answered the door. It was after midnight, and I could tell I'd woken her up. "Gregg," she said. "What are you doing here? I thought it was Steve's turn to come up and see you this weekend."

I told her everything—my cousin knocking on my door for eighteen months, my finally agreeing to go to church with her, the dimly lit room, praying to accept Jesus, the unbelievable peace I felt, and how I knew Steve needed to hear about it from me. When I'd finished, to my surprise, she began to weep. She told me she'd been praying for Steve and me for over a decade. Steve never went to church, so I'd assumed his parents weren't Christians either. But I couldn't have been more wrong.

Steve's mom called his dad to come downstairs, and we sat in the living room together. I told both of them the whole story, and they seemed as blown away as I had felt that night at the church. "I know I have to tell Steve," I exclaimed. "I can't just keep this to myself."

His mom smiled. "You don't know how badly we want to talk to Steve about this ourselves," she said. "And we'd love for him to hear it from you. But you know he won't like it."

"Oh, I know," I said. "I found that out on the phone the other day. But it's the whole reason I came here. You guys go back to bed, and I'm going to wait up for him. I'll try to keep him quiet, but I'm going to talk to him tonight. He needs to hear this from me, and if I try to wait until the morning, I'm not sure if I'll be able to get him to listen."

So, Steve's parents went back upstairs to their room. Maybe they went to bed. But something tells me they stayed up the rest of that night too, praying for us and the conversation we were about to have.

I was tired, and I knew I'd probably fall asleep waiting for

Steve. So, I pushed the couch I was lying on up against the front door, so he wouldn't have a choice but to wake me up. And when he came in about an hour later, I jumped right up to meet him.

Steve was belligerent, just like I knew he would be. I could tell he was coming off a high, and he was not happy to see me. But I grabbed him the way my cousin grabbed me right before she led me back to the dimly lit room. "Look," I said. "I know you don't want to see me. But I have to talk to you. So we're going to go out to the garage, and we're going to talk. Right now."

"No," he said. "I'm going to bed."

"No," I said. "Not yet. Not until after we talk." I could tell he wasn't going to agree on his own. So I grabbed him by the shirt, gripping hard enough that he couldn't get away, and just sort of dragged him out to the garage.

I didn't waste time. "Look, man," I said. "The way we're going, it's not going to be long before we both wind up dead or in jail." Steve and I had been in some close scrapes together—plenty of situations we'd barely gotten out of, whether that meant evading the police or managing to walk away from something that could have killed us. "You know you can't keep living life this way."

"What, and you think going to church is going to suddenly save us from that?" Steve said. "That if I get dressed up and sing some songs on Sunday morning, my life will magically be perfect?" He was mad. I guess I couldn't blame him. But I knew I needed to get his attention, somehow.

"Steve, look," I said. "When I knocked on your door an hour ago, your mom answered. And when I told her that I'd given my life to Jesus, she began to cry, right there in the doorway. She told me that she's been praying for us for over a decade."

Steve softened a bit at this. "I didn't know that."

"I didn't either, man," I said. "But here's what I do know: God is as real as you are to me right now. He spoke to me. He loves us, and He cares about us, and I don't know all the answers to all the questions you probably have, but I do know that I've already seen Him working in my life in just the last five days. I've gotten rid of all the stuff in my house that could keep me from following Him—recreational drugs, alcohol, albums, porn, even cigarettes. I got rid of everything."

"Seriously?" he said. "That's gotta be a thousand dollars' worth of stuff you threw away." I could tell I finally had his full attention.

"This is the most real thing I've ever felt," I said. "And you need it too. You need Jesus. Your mom and dad are probably up praying for us in their room right now. You need to give your life to Jesus right here, right now."

Steve stared at me, and I could see the wheels turning in his mind. Whoever this Jesus was, He was important enough to me that I'd get rid of all my alcohol and drug paraphernalia, drive down two hours to talk to him in the middle of the night, and risk our friendship to tell him all this. His parents had been praying for him for years without ever pressuring him to do anything he didn't want to do. And even if he didn't want to admit it, he knew I was right—if we stayed on the path we'd been on, we were headed for the edge of a cliff.

"Are you sure?" he said.

"I've never been surer of anything in my life," I said.

And, just like I had in that church, Steve said, "Okay."

Right there in his garage, at two in the morning, only five days into following Jesus myself, I led Steve in a prayer to accept Jesus as his Lord and Savior. In just one week, both of our lives were changed forever. And neither of us would ever look back.

CHAPTER 4

Jesus Christ Power and Light

> *"There are two ways to be fooled. One is to believe what isn't true. The other is to refuse to believe what is true."*
>
> –Kierkegaard

STEVE AND I finally went to bed around three in the morning, and we didn't get up until two the next afternoon. We found Steve's parents and his sister Joanne out on the patio, drinking iced tea and enjoying the afternoon air, probably waiting anxiously to hear what had happened last night after Steve got home.

We went out to the patio, and Steve spoke up first. "Well, Dad, Mom—I committed my life to Jesus last night."

That was all he said. And that was all it took. Both of Steve's parents and Joanne began weeping, and those were some of the truest tears of happiness I'd ever seen. They hugged us and told us how thankful and excited they were, how they'd been praying for us for so long. Even now, I feel the emotion of that moment come through every time I tell this story.

It was Saturday, so Steve's parents asked me if I'd stay a little longer so I could go to church with them the next evening. I didn't have any reason to rush home, so I decided to stay, and on Sunday evening I went with them to Fair Oaks Baptist Church in Concord, California.

It was a big church—much bigger than the one I'd been to with Debbie. We walked in and sat down, surrounded by about eight hundred other people. I was a Christian now, but I still felt like a fish out of water. I probably looked like one too—I'm sure Steve and I, walking in with hair down to our shoulders, drew some attention from the regulars.

The church service went on like normal—a few worship songs, a message by the pastor. But then, something happened that I wasn't ready for. After Pastor Carlson finished his sermon, he looked out over the congregation. "I understand," he said, "that we have a couple of young men with us today who just gave their lives to Jesus. Boys, wherever you are, could you please stand up?"

Steve and I looked at each other uncomfortably, hoping that maybe two other people would stand up somewhere else. But it was pretty clear that he was talking about us. So we stood up, looking out at the people around us like a couple of deer caught in headlights.

But the pastor wasn't done. "Boys," he said, "why don't you climb out of your pew and come on up here? I have a few questions I'd like to ask you."

So Steve and I, now fully in shock, crawled out of our pew. We made our way up to the front of the church. And right up there on the stage, in front of a room full of people we'd never met in our lives, the pastor interviewed us. He asked us questions about our lives, where we'd come from, how each of us came to know Jesus, what faith meant to us now, and how we felt our lives had changed. We answered the questions as best we could, not sure whether we were going to get to go back to our seats or if the pastor was going to ask to dunk us in a tank or something.

But then I looked up at the people in the congregation. Everyone was paying attention, transfixed by the stories these two long-haired boys were telling about Jesus coming to meet them. And there wasn't a dry eye in the house.

In that moment, God's power became even more real to me. I knew what I had experienced at Debbie's church that night was real. But here I was, a baby in Christ, standing in front of hundreds of Christians in this church. I had no idea what I was saying. I didn't know anything about the Bible, Jesus, or anything else. And yet, just sharing what God had done in my life clearly had enough power to bring people who already knew Jesus to tears. I had no misconceptions that the emotion sweeping the room had anything to do with me—it was all God.

And it wasn't just emotion. After we were done with our interview and returned to our seats, the pastor did an altar call, inviting anyone in the audience who hadn't accepted Jesus to come forward and give their lives to Him. Steve and I watched in stunned silence as about twenty people left their seats, walked to the front of the room, and committed their lives to Jesus. In a way, their change of heart came from what we had said. But I know it wasn't because of us. God was so evident to me in that moment, and His power came through every word we said.

The church service ended, and I was hit with a wave of exhaustion from everything that had happened over the last few days. I was ready to get back to Steve's house, rest a little bit, and hit the road to go back home. But then I saw someone walk up to me—a tall, pretty girl with long, flowing brown hair. I was tired, but suddenly I felt like I could muster *just* enough energy to talk to her.

"Hi Gregg," she said. "I just wanted to say, wow—that was an amazing testimony. Thank you for sharing it. It was really powerful."

"Thanks," I said. I didn't really know what else to say.

"I'm Janell," she said. "And I had something I wanted to ask you."

I couldn't believe my luck. Not only did I get to see almost twenty people give their lives to Christ after hearing my testimony, but now a beautiful girl was about to ask me out after hearing it too? "Sure," I said. "What is it?"

"Well," she said, "my friend Dennis and I lead the college group here. We call it Jesus Christ Power and Light, and we're meeting in about half an hour. There are about a hundred of us. We wondered if you two might be willing to join us and let us interview you in front of our group, just like you did here this evening at church?"

I suddenly remembered how tired I was. This Janell girl was cute and seemed nice, but actually, it might be even nicer to head back and get some sleep. But somehow, what came out of my mouth was, "Wow, that's nice of you to ask. It's been a long day, but if Steve wants to go, I'll go too."

"Yeah," said Steve. "Yeah, let's do it."

"Great," said Janell. "We'll see you guys there."

About half an hour later, Steve and I showed up in the room where Janell had told us to go. Dimly lit rooms were becoming a bit of a recurring theme for me. The room itself was huge, but the only light was coming from one single candle, right in the middle of the room. I could see a bunch of college-aged people sitting on the floor, but the light was too faint to make out any of their faces. I didn't know what a seance was back then, but if I had, that's probably what it would have reminded me of.

Once the meeting started, it reminded me of a regular church service, but with younger people. Janell's friend Dennis read scripture and shared a message, and everyone sang a few worship songs (which I honestly thought were a little bit weird at the time). Then, Janell stood up.

"Hey everyone, I have Gregg and Steve here with me," she announced. "Guys, I'm going to ask you a few questions. We want to hear your story—anything you want to share."

From there, it was just like what had happened at church a couple of hours earlier. Janell and Dennis asked us questions, and Steve and I shared our testimony: what our lives had been like before, how we came to know Jesus, and the new sense of peace we felt now that we'd never felt before. I couldn't see the audience well enough to tell exactly how everyone was responding to us, but I could tell they were listening closely. And eight college students gave their lives to Christ that night.

Again, this was unreal to me. I was a spiritual newborn, and Steve was even younger in his faith than I was. But here we were, watching people dedicate their lives to Jesus after hearing our story. It felt like God was making His power known to me more and more each day.

By the time we were done, it was ten o'clock, and I was completely wiped out. But Janell and her friend Valerie invited Steve and me to go out for breakfast. All I really wanted to do was get my head to the nearest pillow and go to sleep as soon as possible. But Steve wanted to go to breakfast.

And so, we went to breakfast.

We went to a local place called The Copper Kettle, the only restaurant still open at that hour. I didn't know at the time that, thanks to Steve's insistence on going to breakfast, I was sitting across a breakfast table from Janell (on her birthday!) for the first of many, many times—that it wouldn't be long before we'd be married and have our precious daughter Kaylene, and that one day I'd be writing this book as Janell and I celebrated our fiftieth wedding anniversary. I could have been asleep, but instead, I was sharing my very first meal with my future wife—the love of my life.

Thanks for that one, Steve!

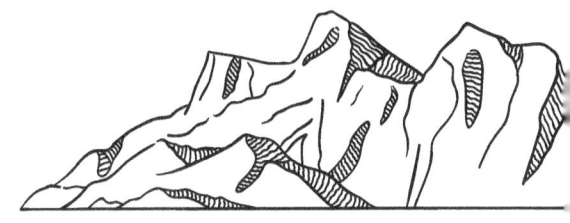

CHAPTER 5

Demons at Ecola Hall

> *"Greater is He who is in you,*
> *than He who is in the world."*
>
> –John 4:4b (NASB)

JUST A FEW weeks later, Steve and I decided together that if we were going to follow Jesus, we had a lot we needed to learn. We were both totally on fire for Jesus, but we also understood how little we actually knew about the Bible.

So, we decided to do something about it.

We heard about a school called Ecola Hall Bible School in Cannon Beach. They offered a one-year program focused on the Old and New Testaments, designed to help students become deeply rooted in their knowledge of scripture. To Steve and me, the program sounded like exactly what we needed. To pay for tuition and living expenses for the next several months, we each sold cars that a few months prior we never would have dreamed of parting with. Steve sold his pristine 1967 Chevelle SS 396, and I sold my 1962 Corvette. It was a fun car, but selling it was one of the best decisions I've ever made.

Ecola Hall provided exactly what Steve and I needed. We were trained in apologetics, hermeneutics, and how to really understand the Old and New Testaments deeply. My faith continued to deepen as I learned more about Jesus, and being around devoted teachers and other students gave me a community of faith like I'd never experienced before.

One of those other students I met at Ecola Hall was named John. John was absolutely brilliant. We all thought he had a photographic memory or some sort of superhuman ability to retain information, because it seemed like whenever one of the Bible teachers gave us a reading assignment, he'd come back next time having memorized every single word. Everyone knew him as a strong Christian and an incredible student.

But Steve and I started experiencing strange things with John—things we didn't expect to come from a fellow student at a Bible college. The first time we noticed something was off, we were sitting around discussing what we'd been learning and experiencing in our own lives. I started sharing a story about what I'd been learning about Jesus and how I'd been experiencing His power in my life, and then I looked at John.

He was glaring at me. I did a double take, and as I continued talking, it seemed like John was caught somewhere between intense anger and extreme discomfort. He didn't say anything, but he looked like he hated every word that was coming out of my mouth. He was squirming, and there was fire behind his eyes.

We noticed this strange reaction multiple times when we talked about Jesus around John. Every time, he would glare at us like he was angry at us for bringing up Jesus, which seemed odd to us at a Bible college. And even though Steve and I, along with everyone else, had assumed John was a Christian, he started bringing things up to us that would challenge our belief in God and His power. He was clearly trying to plant seeds of doubt in our minds, but we had no idea why another follower of Jesus would want to do that.

That wasn't all, though. John started doing more than just talking to us—he started actively trying to pull us into compromising situations that he knew would challenge our faith. He knew that we were young believers, and it started to seem like it was his goal to destroy our faith in Jesus and put us in positions that would pull us straight back into the lives we were living before. He invited us to participate in things I never would have thought possible for a student at a Bible college.

This went on for the first few months or so of my time at Ecola Hall. Then I learned that a pastor named Ray Stedman was going to be visiting campus to speak. Ray didn't really know me, but I knew who he was. He was a pastor in Palo Alto, and he did a lot of work with Stanford students. Janell and I had gone over to hear him speak a few times, and I'd actually met him. I also knew that his associate pastor, Ron Ritchie, was the man who discipled Janell's father.

All of this led me to trust Ray, and for some reason, I felt like he was the one we needed to talk to about John. So, after Ray finished teaching, Steve and I walked up to the front of the room to talk to him. We introduced ourselves, and then we shared everything that had been happening—the ways John reacted when we talked about Jesus, the things he'd been saying to us, and the sinful activities he'd been trying to pull us into.

Ray looked me square in the face. "This young man is possessed," he said. "We need to get him in a room together so we can help him."

Steve and I were shocked, but we could tell Ray was serious. So, we went and found John, and we told him we needed to talk to him. He followed us, and we led him into a room where Ray and a couple of other mature Christians were waiting for us. We closed the door.

"John," Ray said, "we're going to pray for you. You're going to experience freedom tonight."

Immediately, John's eyes changed. I could see the same look of intense hatred we saw every time we talked to him about Jesus. But Ray didn't hesitate. He started praying, along with the others in the room, and Steve and I joined in. We all prayed for John together. Ray addressed the demons directly, demanding that they come out of him in the name of Jesus.

And one by one, they began to come out. It was like nothing Steve or I had ever seen. John's body became as limp as a rag doll. He was thrown across the room, and several of us grabbed him to hold him still and keep him from getting hurt. It was all we could do to hold him down as the demons fled his body. It was like an invisible force was pulling him, contorting his body in unnatural ways. I've experienced some hard, scary things, but I'm not exaggerating when I tell you that the hour we spent in that room with John was one of the worst hours of my life.

And then, John's body relaxed. The demons were gone. John looked up at us, and then at Ray, and the hateful look in his eyes had completely changed. His body was relaxed, and we could tell just by looking at him that he was at total peace. I realized that it was probably the first peace John had experienced in a very long time.

"John," Ray said, "the power of Jesus saved you today. He gave you freedom from the demons that were oppressing you, but He wants to do more than that. He wants to give you freedom forever. He wants to be your Savior, your Lord, and your friend. Will you give your life over to Him today?"

Without hesitating, John said, "Okay." And Ray led him in a prayer to accept Jesus into his life.

We all experienced something life-changing in that room on that day. John experienced freedom—first from the demons that had been oppressing him, and then the kind of eternal freedom that Jesus offers. After that day, John was a different person. He remained a student at Ecola Hall, and he finished the rest of the year, growing in his walk with God and committed to helping others find the freedom he had experienced himself. John went on to become the pastor of an evangelical church in Portland, Oregon.

For me, what I saw in that room changed my perspective on the God Whom I'd still only been following for a few months. I obviously believed that God was real, and I knew that He was powerful. I'd read things in the Bible about how God's power was stronger than Satan's power. But experiencing it firsthand—seeing demons flee at the very mention of Jesus's name—helped me understand it in a whole new way.

I saw God's power that day up close and personal. All the things I'd read and heard—that God is mighty to save, that His strength is unshakeable, that there is no one in heaven or on earth powerful enough to overcome Him or His majestic angels—I saw these truths with my own eyes. I saw both fallen angels and what I like to call "Navy Seal" or "Army Ranger" angels—God's secret agents—at work, right there in front of me. And while I've never experienced anything else quite like what I saw that day, it wouldn't be the last time I experienced God's power to rescue someone from death.

And plenty of times, that someone would be me.

CHAPTER 6

Five Prayers at Biola

> *"The prayers of men and women move the hands of God."*
>
> –UNKNOWN

AFTER WE FINISHED our year at Ecola Hall, Steve and I were recruited to work at a Christian camp called Miracle Ranch in Port Orchard, Washington. I loved the idea of putting my faith into practice by investing in young kids using the outdoor skills that I'd gained over the course of my life.

Steve and I both worked as counselors at Miracle Ranch, and I taught sailing, water skiing, and horsemanship. There were about forty horses at the camp, and I got to teach kids how to ride and take them out on trails. I started learning worship songs on my guitar too, and I helped lead worship at the camp. I'd come a long way from sitting in that dark room at Jesus Christ Power and Light, wondering what was with the strange songs these people were singing. It was an amazing summer, and we saw hundreds of young people make life-changing decisions to commit their lives to Jesus.

I also got to see my mother and my sister Michelle pray to accept Jesus as their Savior when they came to visit me. I had encouraged them to come, and when they did, they accepted Jesus and made commitments to serve Him as Lord of their lives. Michelle was a real cowgirl, and she went on to help plant cowboy churches and serve in women's ministries until her life tragically ended in a head-on collision with a young driver who was asleep at the wheel. I'm forever grateful that I had the chance to see her come to know Jesus.

About halfway through the summer, Miracle Ranch hosted a guest speaker named Lance. Lance was a dynamic teacher, and as I got to know him during his time visiting the camp, I quickly developed a strong admiration and respect for him.

My dear sister.

He committed time to getting to know me too, even taking me sailing on his thirty-eight-foot sailboat around the San Juan Islands, just off the coast of Washington.

When I met Lance, my mindset about my faith had changed, but my dreams for my future career hadn't—I still imagined myself flying for the US Forest Service or working in the sporting goods and ski industry. But Lance challenged me. He told me that I needed to open myself up to the idea that God might be preparing me for full-time ministry, and that if I was serious about following Jesus, I needed to pray about that and be open to going wherever God might lead me.

That conversation was a significant moment for me. I was committed to my faith, but up to this point I'd never imagined myself as more than someone who would minister to people wherever I could in the context of whatever work I might be doing. To hear from Lance, someone who was ministering to people full-time and had such great wisdom and experience, that he saw that same potential in me—that really shifted my mindset toward what my life could look like.

So, I did what Lance encouraged me to do: I prayed. I asked God that if He wanted me to dedicate my life to full-time ministry, He would make it clear and show me the next step.

As the rest of the summer unfolded, I began to feel a change in my heart. I started sensing that God was calling me to full-time ministry, as Lance suggested, and that He was preparing me for my next step. I just didn't know what that next step was.

Well, that lack of clarity didn't last long. As it turned out, there was an opening for a high school ministry intern at Walnut Creek Presbyterian Church in the Bay Area—the church where Janell's father worked as a pastor of evangelism. I learned about the opportunity and reached out to the church, and ultimately, they offered me the internship. About a year into my own personal walk with God, I went to work with high school students as a youth minister.

In a lot of ways, the position was like a continuation of my time at Miracle Ranch. I was working in a church instead of guiding campers on horseback trail rides, but I was still working with high schoolers, which I had loved so much at camp. I had the chance to make an impact on so many students, and during my time there, God blessed our ministry with incredible growth. We saw so many teenagers grow in their faith and deepen their walks with God as we spent time together in the church and on adventures— backpacking trips, bike trips, ski trips, and mountaineering expeditions. My friend Barry and I repurposed his two-and-a-half-ton, six-by-six army troop transport truck into the perfect vehicle to take these kids wherever we wanted to go. We also took kids on six-week trips to British Columbia to build a Christian youth camp for the North American Indian Mission. It was all new, exciting, and life-giving to my heart—God was giving me the opportunity to minister to young people while also building in them an appreciation for adventure and His creation, all things that have been dear to my heart for my entire life.

God used my time at Walnut Creek Presbyterian Church to affirm what I had begun feeling at Miracle Ranch: He was calling me to ministry. But I also sensed a more specific call. Many of the people encouraging me to a life of ministry thought I should become a pastor. But I was feeling called to something else: dedicating my life to camp ministry. God wasn't calling me to plant churches. He was calling and pre-paring me to plant camps.

I served for a few years in church ministry, but as I shared more with some of the pastors there about where I sensed God was leading me, they encouraged me to pursue a college degree that would train and prepare me to step into that calling. They recognized my strong passion for evangelism and discipleship and my love for using the great outdoors as a springboard to teach life skills and biblical principles to young people.

It just so happened that I knew of a place that offered just the kind of degree I was looking for. Steve's sister Joanne had told me during our time at Miracle Ranch about the college she attended, Biola University. Biola stood for Bible Institute of Los Angeles, and they were launching a new degree pro-gram in Christian camping and recreation administration. There was no doubt in my mind that this was the right place— exactly the next step that God was leading me to.

Janell and I were married on October 5, 1974, and shortly after our wedding, I enrolled at Biola and we moved together to La Mirada, California. I prayed for five specific things at the start of our time there:

1. That I would find a strong Christian professor who would take me under his wing.
2. That we would find an affordable place to live close to campus.
3. That I would find a job where I could apply what I was learning about Christian camping ministry.

4. That Janell would find a job that would allow us to see each other when I wasn't at school or at work.
5. That we'd find a great church to attend.

And if I had any questions about whether this was the right place for us to be, they were quickly erased when I saw God's responses to each of my prayers.

October 5, 1974: the BEST day of my life!

We hadn't even been at Biola a week when I met Dr. Bill Bynum. He was the head of Christian Education at Talbott Seminary, which was affiliated with Biola and located on the same campus. He was teaching a group dynamics course that I wanted to take, even though I wasn't enrolled in the seminary and hadn't signed up for the class. I showed up on the first night of the course to ask Dr. Bynum about it, and he told me I couldn't take the class because it was full. The course was built around the students working in groups of three and forming close personal relationships as they moved through the coursework together, and the class was already evenly divided into groups of three. So, I asked him if I could just sit in the back of the room and observe, and he agreed.

I showed up for every class, and for the first two weeks, I just sat quietly in the back of the room and watched the rest of the class participate in their groups of three. But halfway through the third week, Dr. Bynum called me. "Gregg," he said, "one of my students dropped out. If you're still interested in taking the class, there's a spot for you now. You're in."

I was grateful that I was able to take the class. But what I didn't realize at that moment was that this was God answering the first of my prayers: that I would find a strong Christian professor to take me under his wing. My friendship with Dr. Bynum started during this course, and ultimately he would become a spiritual father to me. He was an amazing man of God, a great friend, and a generous mentor. I don't think I would have made it through my time at Biola without him.

God couldn't have been more kind in His answer to the first of my five prayers.

There was an apartment complex a block away from Biola's campus that Janell and I thought would be a perfect place for us to live while I was in school. It was a nice apartment complex—nicer than we'd probably be able to afford on our own. But when we went to see it, we decided to apply to live there anyway, and when we spoke to the complex owner he told us that his manager was leaving and that if we'd like to manage the apartment complex, we could live there without paying rent. We agreed with no hesitation—God had answered my second prayer.

Answers to the third and fourth prayers—that God would provide the right jobs for Janell and me—came quickly as well. Janell found a job in the financial aid office on campus, which was great for two reasons. First, it meant that generally, we were both on the same schedule. She worked while I was at school, which allowed us to spend time together during our "off" hours. And second, being in the financial aid office gave her great visibility to the scholarships that were available. She was able to help me apply for any scholarships that I qualified for, which was a huge help to us financially.

As for me, thanks to my experience working in Christian camping settings before coming to Biola, I was able to get a job teaching and writing curriculum in the Christian Camping and Recreation Administration department. I taught three levels of canoeing, backpacking, and survival courses, sharing the knowledge I had gained on not just the skills, but how to

*Graduation day alongside
Kaylene and my bride.*

use these activities to form relationships with young people and teach them about the Bible. I also served as a "Mountain Minister" with Summit Bound guiding backpacking, canoeing, rafting, rock climbing, and ski trips in the Sierra Nevada Mountains near Yosemite National Park. I loved every minute of it, and just like I had prayed, it was a way for me to put into practice what I was learning at Biola.

My fifth prayer was that we would find a strong church to attend, and the answer to that started when Chuck Swindoll visited our campus to speak at an event. I listened to him speak, and afterwards I was able to meet him. I was so impressed with him that Janell and I decided to visit his church, Fullerton Evangelical Free. We knew right away that it was the right place for us, and we attended there throughout our time at Biola. Fullerton Evangelical Free provided exactly what we needed in a church and a wonderful answer from God to the fifth prayer I had prayed.

God had called me to Biola. He answered all five of the prayers I prayed when Janell and I arrived there. And He was faithful to me throughout my time there, from the first day I enrolled to when I graduated in 1980. He gave me so many opportunities to grow and learn the skills I'd need to step into the calling He'd laid on my heart. I didn't know exactly what path He was going to lead me down next. But I was completely convinced that Biola was the right place to be, exactly how God wanted to equip me for the work He'd prepared for me to do next.

CHAPTER 7

Colorado to Branson

> *"When God opens a door, it is often an exit from our comfort zone."*
>
> –DAVID JEREMIAH

DURING MY TIME at Biola, I was asked to represent the university at the Christian Camping International Conference in French Lick, Indiana. And that's where I first met Joe White.

In 1976, Joe began serving as president of Kanakuk Kamps. As I write this book, Joe continues to serve as CEO of Kanakuk Ministries, which has been operating in Missouri since 1926 and has welcomed nearly half a million campers since its founding. He has provided leadership at Kanakuk for decades, and he is the founder of Kids Across America (KAA) Kamps. Joe is a prolific speaker and author, having written more than twenty books. Dr. James Dobson, founder of Focus on the Family, claims that Joe White knows more about teenagers than anyone else in America. When I first met him, I knew he represented such a great example of the kind of camp ministry leadership I hoped to grow into over the course of my life.

And on top of all that, he made one heck of a first impression.

I was standing in the middle of the conference center at the Christian Camping International Conference, and I started hearing lots of commotion on the other side of the room. I looked over, and I saw the source right away: a group of guys going crazy on roller skates, gliding and laughing their way through the conference center. And right at the front of the group was Joe, leading his people as only he could. He and his entourage of fun-loving directors were roller skating through the inside halls and outside paths of French Lick's prestigious conference center.

That was pretty much all it took for me to see that Joe White was a man's man, and my kind of guy. I made it a point to meet him in person at the conference (after his team was asked to leave with their roller skates, of course). Several years later, I invited him to come speak at our church's annual family camp. That started a friendship with Joe that I knew would continue for years to come. But I never could have anticipated the full impact his friendship would have on my life, or the way his example of dynamic Christian leadership would shape me.

After graduating from Biola in 1980, I moved with Janell to Buena Vista, Colorado. I had been recruited there to convert Mount Princeton Hot Springs Resort into a Christian camp and conference center. After that, I was recruited to give direction and serve at Horn Creek Christian Conference Center, which included three different camps, two for youth and one for families.

After my time working at Horn Creek, we moved to Denver, where I was recruited to give direction to the Campus Life division of Denver Area Youth for Christ. During my time there, we established vibrant evangelistic and discipleship-minded club ministries on more than thirty junior high and high school campuses in the greater Denver metro area, and my experience working with teenagers through camps prepared me to help serve in this ministry, working with club directors to effectively connect to kids through their school environments.

Eventually, I was asked to come work with the president of Youth for Christ USA in the national office, which had moved to Denver. I primarily served in the area of advancement and stewardship ministry. I was blessed to come alongside and encourage executive directors and contributors all across the country, painting our vision and mission for them, encouraging them, and helping them develop a master plan for their local ministries.

Janell and I loved just about everything about our time with Youth for Christ. I loved my job, knowing that the work I was doing was impacting tens of thousands of teenagers every year across the nation who so desperately needed the hope of Jesus. We loved living in Denver, close to cultural opportunities for our family but still near enough to the mountains that we were able to spend plenty of time enjoying the incredible recreational opportunities the Rockies provided. And we absolutely loved our church, which we had helped to plant and establish. God had blessed it, and we got to watch it grow from forty people in the first four weeks to four hundred in the first four months and four thousand in the first four years. Janell and I co-led a Koinonia Bible study group with six other amazing couples, and I was asked early on to serve as the elder of family and youth. It was an incredible community for our family to be a part of. If given the choice, there really wasn't much about our life that we would change.

And, of course, that's when Joe White called.

The phone rang one day, and I heard Joe's voice on the other end. His call wasn't too unusual—we had maintained a friendship over the years. But I had never expected to hear the words that came out of his mouth.

"Gregg," he said. "I need to talk to you about moving to Branson, Missouri. We need you to come alongside us and help provide leadership for our urban camping ministry, Kids Across America Kamps."

I almost laughed. "Joe, there's no way," I said. "There's no way in heaven we could ever make a move like that. We're so rooted here. I love my work with Youth for Christ USA, and they need me. Janell, Kaylene, and I have such a wonderful community at our church, and Kaylene is still in high school. There's no way I could imagine that God would uproot and pull my family away from what we have here in Denver."

"Listen, Gregg," Joe said. "We need someone with your experience and background, and our board doesn't want anybody else. We want you."

"Joe, I just can't," I said. "I'm sorry. I can't." I explained to Joe that I was committed to my dear friend Roger Cross, president of Youth For Christ USA, and our pastor at Cherry Creek Presbyterian Church, Mark Brewer. And Ken and Jeanne Atkinson, our dearest friends in the world, had just had two children diagnosed with a fatal blood disease. I told Joe with finality, "I'm just not in a position to come."

I had given Joe a clear answer. But he must not have heard me, because he called me again a few weeks later. He was praying for me and continued to call as the Lord brought me

My treasured friend Ken Atkinson and me.

to his mind for several months, and we did the same dance every time. He would tell me they needed me in Branson. I'd tell him I couldn't imagine leaving Denver. He'd tell me God could really use me to give direction at Kids Across America. I'd tell him I was too deeply rooted in Colorado. And then he'd pray for me, and he'd ask me to pray and consider the opportunity he was offering me to help our nation's urban young people. And then we'd both hang up, knowing that we'd be having the same conversation again in the near future.

During this time, I went to a Promise Keepers pastors conference in Atlanta where Dr. Tony Evans was speaking. Some eleven thousand ministry leaders attended, and Dr. Evans challenged all of us on the final night of the conference. He asked every one of us men to get down on our knees, and he called for complete silence in the room. He challenged us not to get up until we'd told God what we were holding back from Him. "God doesn't want 95 percent, or 98 percent, or even 99 percent," Dr. Evans said emphatically. "He wants it all."

So, I got down on my knees. I was down there for five minutes, and I truly couldn't think of a single thing. I was up to my eyebrows in ministry, and I had a great church, a great family. Everything was great. I was blessed beyond measure, and I couldn't think of anything I was holding back from God because—why would I?

I got up off my knees, the conference ended, and I headed back home to Denver. I never really figured out the answer to Dr. Evans's question.

But when I got back home, something strange started happening. Everywhere I went, I started seeing Kanakuk. I saw Kanakuk brochures on friends' dining room tables. Kanakuk bumper stickers on cars I'd drive by. People from Kanakuk at random places. It felt ridiculous—I was being bombarded by Kanakuk from two states away.

"I'm going to send you plane tickets," Joe said to me in one of our phone calls. "Just fly out to visit Branson and see the camps. We can talk about what it would be like for you to work here."

"Joe," I said, "please don't send tickets. I can't come! We have twenty-two thousand kids coming to a conference in Washington, D.C., and then another twelve thousand coming to a conference in LA this summer, and I just can't."

At this point, it had been over a year since Joe had started calling about Kanakuk, and I still hadn't told Janell, or anyone else for that matter. It wasn't because I was planning anything in secret. I just didn't want to worry her or make her think I was actually considering it, because I truly wasn't. But I was beginning to wonder if the real reason I was holding back was because I didn't want to leave our comfort zone in Colorado.

I decided to confide in our dear friends Jack and Martha Carter, whose daughter Rachel attended Kanakuk Kamps, because I knew they had a lot of respect for Joe White. I told them about the opportunity to serve with Kids Across America Kamps. They encouraged me to not hold back, to seriously consider the possibility, and to pray with Janell about it.

Long-time friends Jack and Martha Carter with their daughter, Rachel.

So, I did. I shared with Janell that Joe had been calling me periodically for over a year, and I told her what he had been challenging me to consider. She reacted how I had guessed she would.

"No way," she said. "Not a chance. We can't move."

"That's what I had thought too," I said. "The thought of moving makes me bristle! I honestly haven't even prayed about it because it never seemed like an option. We have too much going on here. But they just keep calling and calling, every few weeks. Even a corporate recruiter from Colorado Springs is calling me. And I've started thinking more about what Dr. Evans said at that conference—God wants 100 percent. And I wonder if not being open to the possibility of moving is the last 2 percent that I'm keeping from Him.

"Janell," I questioned, "would you be willing to at least pray to see if God might want to move us from Denver to Branson? I'm not asking this because I want to go. But at this point, I think we should make sure God doesn't want us to go before we just decide we're not going."

"Well, I'll pray about it," she said. "But I just don't see how Branson could possibly be where God wants us to go." I was so amazed and grateful to hear her say those words. It was such an unexpected, huge step of faith for Janell.

That evening, we got down on our knees next to our bed, and I prayed a simple prayer. "God," I said, "if this is something you want me to pursue, you're going to have to open this door so wide that I can't help but tumble through it." That was it. But it was the first moment that I had truly opened my heart to the possibility of moving to Branson, if that's what God wanted. And from that moment, God started working, and both of our hearts began to change.

Eventually, I called Joe back. "Okay," I said. "If you want me to fly in, I'll fly in. I'll be in Seattle for some meetings in three weeks, and I could come in from there. But you'll also need to fly Janell in from Denver and Kaylene in from Westmont College in Santa Barbara. This is a major decision, and I need both of them to be a part of it too."

I could almost hear Joe smiling on the other end of the phone. "Done," he said. "See you in three weeks."

Three weeks later, Janell, Kaylene, and I all converged in Springfield, Missouri, where Bruce, one of the Kids Across America directors, picked us up and drove us to Joe's office.

At long last, Joe's prayers were being favorably answered: the chance to sit me down and talk to me in person, to convince me that I needed to come and provide leadership for the ministry of Kids Across America. I had prepared myself for this moment. I took a deep breath and sat down, ready to hear what Joe had to say to me.

And so, of course, Joe proceeded to mostly ignore me for the next hour.

He and one of his assistants spent the entire first hour of our time together focused completely on Janell and Kaylene. He asked them questions, listened to their concerns, and spent a lot of time working to convince them that this wasn't just the place where I needed to be—it was the place where *we* needed to be. I could tell how much that meant to them, and it meant a lot to me too.

The Kanakuk and Kids Across America Kamps leaders were kind, thoughtful, and caring to us throughout our visit. Joe knew that I owned and loved riding horses, and he arranged to have me tour the Kids Across America Kamps property on horseback with their CFO Don, who also owned horses. They also took us to dinner at Big Cedar Lodge and treated us to Silver Dollar City, a local amusement park. I had never been to Branson. Before this trip, I barely knew where it was. Being from California and having lived in Colorado for so many years, I knew that moving here would feel a bit like moving to Africa for our family. But Joe and his team did everything they could to help us imagine a positive life in Branson.

They set us up with nice lodging at the infamous Sammy Lane Resort on Taneycomo Lake, just a mile or so from camp. Our cabin balcony extended out over the cool, beautiful waterfront. Both late nights, after very full days, I could hear Janell and Kaylene giggling on their beds as I was getting out of the shower. When I came out and sat down, much to my chagrin, they both began trying to convince me that KAA really needed me and that I was the right person to provide the leadership for it. So I told them they needed to keep praying, and they did.

The last morning of our visit, I got up at 5:00 a.m., sat on the balcony and opened to Psalm 41. The first words I read were, "Blessed are those who have regard for the weak; the Lord delivers them in times of trouble. The Lord protects and preserves them—they are counted among the blessed in the land."

I knew in those early morning moments that God was speaking directly to me through His Holy Word. I quietly prayed, "Okay God, I hear you loud and clear. Here I am. However, Lord, I don't have the strength and power to do this. It has to be you filling me with your Holy Spirit. This is your camp, and I surrender to your calling. Also, God, please begin even now to prepare the hearts and minds of all those we will be abandoning back in Colorado. Give them peace and understanding when we announce your calling on our lives to depart for the ministry of Kids Across America Kamps in Branson."

I knew with growing conviction that this was where we were supposed to be. Janell and Kaylene knew it too. And so,

I accepted the position of president for Kids Across America, a role I would fill for nearly twenty years. Even in the years following the position, I've been blessed to continue to work with Kanakuk, connecting with friends and serving in stewardship ministry.

I never could have imagined leaving Denver. I certainly never could have imagined moving to Branson. But as soon as I opened myself up to God, it wasn't long at all before I realized that this was exactly where He wanted me to be. He's been present and faithful in my time with KAA in ways beyond my wildest imagination.

Every dream I've had since my call to camp ministry fifty years ago until now has been fulfilled. And from the day I accepted the position until this day, as I write this book, every single moment of every single day, I've been overwhelmed with the sense that, by God's grace, I've been right in the middle of where He wants me.

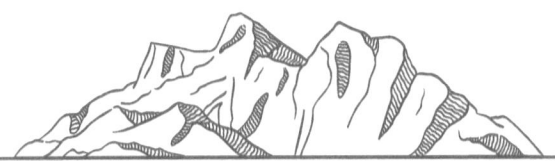

PART TWO

Into the Unknown

*"Faith isn't faith…
until it's all you're
holding onto."*

–KENOL POLICARD

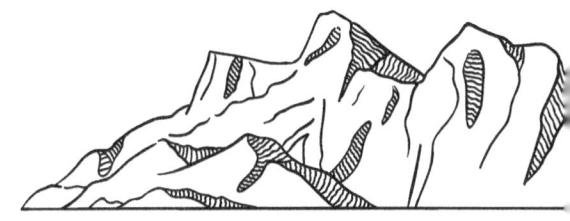

CHAPTER 8

An Early Landing

*"There are old pilots, and there are bold
pilots, but there are no old bold pilots."*

–HARRY D. COPELAND

ONE MORNING IN 2004, about six years into
my time at Kids Across America, I left for a trip I
had scheduled to meet with some dear contributor
friends in California. I was piloting myself, so I got up early
in the morning and took off from Branson. I was in the air
by five in the morning.

When I took longer trips like this one, I always made it
a point to stop and visit friends along the way. So, my first
stop was Amarillo, Texas, for a breakfast meeting. Then,
I flew to Albuquerque, New Mexico, for a lunch meeting.
Both meetings were great, and I was still on track to be in
California by dinnertime.

As I prepared to leave Albuquerque for my final destination, things started to get interesting. It was February, so temperatures were already cold, but while I was in Albuquerque it started snowing to beat the band. So, much to my chagrin, shortly after takeoff I encountered rime icing and had to climb high enough that I'd be able to fly without battling ice. I was at twelve thousand feet when suddenly, without warning, my airplane started porpoising, wildly rocking up and down.

The timing wasn't great. It would be getting dark soon, and I knew I'd be flying over the southern Sierra mountain range and into San Diego airspace, which would be busy with other aircraft. But after I switched off autopilot and began hand-flying the plane, it calmed down. I was back in control.

After flying manually for a little while, I decided to try switching it back to autopilot. Almost immediately, the plane started porpoising wildly again, and I knew that auto-pilot was going to be a no-go for this flight. I switched back to flying manually, this time for good.

I was only an hour out from my destination of San Diego when Los Angeles Center Control made contact with me. The air traffic controller came on the radio and instructed me to descend and maintain ten thousand feet. But that was a problem—I was flying higher to stay above the icing, and lowering to ten thousand feet would put me right in the middle of it. I needed to stay where I was to keep everything on my plane from freezing up completely. I tried to respond by radio to the air traffic controller to let them know I couldn't do what they were asking because of the weather.

And that's when everything went dark.

My instrument panel completely lost power. I had zero navigational instruments except for a magnetic compass. I had no lights, no attitude indicator, no radio—I had nothing. Even my paper maps were in the back of the plane, and since I was flying manually, I couldn't reach them.

So, there I was, with zero ability to communicate and a lot of icing between me and the ground. I didn't know where I was going to break out of the icing—it could be at five thousand feet, or maybe five hundred feet, or maybe fifty feet. I had no idea. I decided that I would head down as the air traffic controller had suggested, but I wasn't going to stop at ten thousand feet—I'd pick up too much ice.

I began my descent. I went down past ten thousand, down past five thousand. I went all the way down to about 2,200 feet above the ground, and I finally broke out of the clouds and icing. I breathed a small sigh of relief, but I had picked up a significant amount of ice during my descent—nearly two inches of it. And then my engine started cutting out. I didn't realize it at the time, but as I rapidly flew down through the icing I had super cooled the engine—it wasn't getting enough aspirated air to be able to run properly.

At this point, I was about two thousand feet above the ground, and my engine was still cutting in and out. I started thinking I was going to have to ditch my plane in the middle of the desert. Thankfully, as I continued under the icing, sublimation began melting the ice, and the engine began to improve enough for me to continue.

But that was the end of the good news. I was supposed to be heading west toward San Diego, which would take me over the Chocolate Mountains, but I didn't feel great about flying over the mountains without radio, lights, or navigation aids. So, I decided to change plans. I knew if I headed north instead of west, I'd probably run into Interstate 40, which would help lead me to El Centro Naval Air Force Base and Marine Corp Training Facilities. They had long, wide runways, and I thought it would be a good place for me to safely get on the ground as soon as possible.

Of course, that was all assuming I could find El Centro before the military found me. I knew I was flying through highly restricted airspace. I had clearance, but if they found me wandering off my clearance—as I was about to do— they'd either shoot me down or, if I were lucky, force me to the ground. And if they found me, I'd have no way to communicate with them and let them know that I was in an emergency mode of operation.

I silently thanked God when I found I-40. I followed it east until I was about ten miles out on a final approach into El Centro Naval Weapons Base, and then my heart froze. An F-18 flew directly over the top of me, no more than a thousand feet above my position.

I held my breath as the F-18 continued its glide path to the runway. Thankfully, the pilot hadn't seen me. But that moment made one thing even clearer to me: I had to get out of there.

I immediately peeled off and landed on an east-west runway. Directly in front of me was a harrier attack jet taxiing on a crosswind runway, which could mean only one thing—he saw me too. Almost immediately, the tower flashed a red signal at me. I knew what that signal meant: stop where you are, and shut down your engine. I knew if I turned it off, I wouldn't be able to get it started again, but I had no other choice. I stopped, powered down the engine, and waited.

I didn't have to wait long. The entire base lit up like a fireworks factory. Within two or three minutes, I was completely surrounded by what seemed to be about a hundred reconnaissance vehicles. Some of them had .50 caliber machine guns attached to them. I knew they were discussing what to do, trying to figure out who I was and what in the world I was doing in their airspace. For all they knew, I could have been transporting bombs or drugs.

I sat there for at least half an hour until, finally, two of the reconnaissance vehicles pulled forward. Four dogs jumped out of the vehicles and started smelling all around my airplane. They ran around every side, jumped up on my wings, and after they had smelled everything, they were called back. About five more minutes passed, and then one of the vehicles approached my plane, coming within about fifty feet of me.

"Keep your hands in the air where we can see them at all times," a man called through his bullhorn. "Get out of your airplane and lie spread-eagle on the ground."

I had no intention of doing anything other than exactly what was asked of me. I held up my hands, carefully worked my way out of the plane, stepped down onto the freezing ground, and lay down with my arms and legs extended. I stayed there, silent and motionless, for twenty minutes. Finally, a man who I'd soon learn was the commander of the base walked up to me.

"Mr. Bettis," he said, "I'm very sorry we've had to detain you like this, but we didn't know who you were, where you were from, or what your intentions were." They had taken the time to research my identity before I ever stepped off the plane.

"That's okay," I said. "I lost my power, my panel went dark at altitude, and I lost touch with LA Center Control. I wasn't able to communicate with anyone."

He nodded. "Yes, we got in touch with LA Center, and they told us they had lost communication with you. They didn't know what had happened or if you were even alive. We told them that you were safely on the ground here. But before we could let you leave, we had to make sure we knew who you were and where you were going."

I nodded, and the commander seemed to notice that I was still lying spread-eagle on the ground. "Oh—you can get up now, Mr. Bettis," he said. "Listen, we're happy to do whatever we can to help you. But your plane has to be out of here by 7:00 a.m. tomorrow, or else it will have to be detained here for the next thirty days. We're working on a highly classified project, and you can't be on the base."

I stood up and brushed myself off. "No problem. I think my alternator has gone bad. If you can just tow my little plane to a hangar and put it on a battery charger, I think it'll be okay. Then I'll fly it to San Diego or a neighboring airport."

He nodded. "We can do that."

"But right now, sir," I sighed, "I'm just exhausted. It's been a full day, and once we get my plane on a charger, I just need to get to a hotel and get some sleep. I'll get up early in the morning to get here and fly it out."

"I understand," he said. "We'll transport you to the hotel and pick you up in the morning to come back."

They towed the plane to a hangar, where we were able to get it attached to a charger. I was struck by the humor of the image I was looking at—my tiny little airplane, all alone in this enormous military hangar. But more than anything, I felt completely wiped out. Although I was grateful that things had worked out as well as they had, at that moment I wanted nothing more than to collapse into the first hotel bed I could find.

But as we were finishing up with my airplane, someone walked over to us out of the hangar office. "Mr. Bettis," they said. "I'm afraid we can't let you leave just yet. The captain of the tower would like to speak with you immediately."

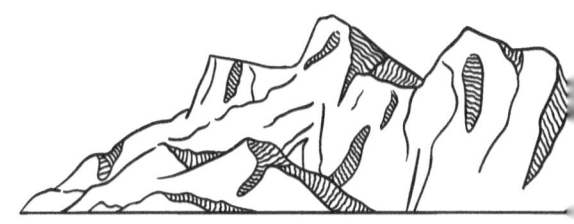

CHAPTER 9

Right Place, Right Time

> *"Do what is right. Right what
> is wrong. And speak truth."*
>
> –UNKNOWN

I HELD MY BREATH as the commander drove me over to the base of the tower. I didn't know what was about to happen. Maybe they just wanted to ask me more questions. Maybe they were planning to detain me or suspend my pilot's license. Either way, my long day clearly wasn't over yet.

We got to the base of the tower early in the evening, just as the sun was setting. A man was standing there waving at us. As I stepped out of the commander's vehicle, he signaled for me to follow him, so I did. We walked into the base of the massive tower, got into an elevator, and went straight to the top.

When we got out of the elevator, the captain pointed at a long paper ticket that was taped to the edge of a countertop that wrapped all the way around the room. The paper was seventeen inches wide, and probably 150 feet long. He looked at me. "Gregg, do you see this ticket?" he said. "That's your entire life."

I looked at it, amazed. They seemed to have just about every piece of information about me that existed. They had pictures of me on the ground in my airplane in Columbus, Ohio, from two weeks earlier. They knew who my kindergarten teacher was. They knew who I was married to, where I'd gone to school, every job I'd ever had. He was right—my entire life was right there on that ticket.

I wondered if somehow they'd found something about me that, combined with my unexpected landing on their restricted base, had given them cause for concern. Was he showing me this to try to throw me off balance? Was he trying to intimidate me?

"Gregg," the captain said. "I know you're exhausted. But I'd like to take you for a ride. Please follow me."

I nodded. I was exhausted, but obviously I didn't have a choice. So I followed him down to his pickup truck, and we started driving away from the base.

After we'd been in his truck for about five minutes, the captain looked over at me. "Gregg," he said. "You know that I know who you are. I know you're a Christian. I know you've been involved in ministry for a long time and impacted thousands of people's lives."

I stared at him, silent. This is not what I was expecting.

"I became a Christian two years ago," he continued. "My wife and kids are still not Christians, and they won't come to church with me. My wife also has a best friend who lives across the street, and she isn't a believer either. But the couple who lives next to us are believers, and they're the ones who led me to Christ. We've all been praying for my family and my wife's friend for a long time. And I'm wondering if God sent you here tonight for a reason.

"Would you be willing to come home with me tonight?" he asked. "Would you be willing to share your story with my wife and neighbors? We'd love to put you up at our house tonight. We'll feed you a delicious dinner, and we've got a nice guest room you can stay in."

I was so tired at this point it was hard to imagine staying awake through dinner, let alone sharing my story with this man's wife and neighbors. But I couldn't deny that there was a chance he was right—maybe God did have me here tonight for a reason.

"Sure," I said. "Sounds great."

He thanked me, and then he pulled out his cell phone as he continued driving. "Hey," he said when his wife answered, "I'm on my way home, and I'm bringing a pilot with me who had a forced landing at the base. He's going to be having dinner and spending the night with us. He's got a very interesting story, and I asked him to share it with us after dinner. Call the neighbors and invite them too—we can all eat dinner together and then spend the evening out by the fire pit."

We arrived at the captain's house. He introduced me to his wife and neighbors, and we all sat down to eat dinner. As tired as I was, I hadn't realized that I was hungry too. The food was great, and it was nice to have a good meal after the day I'd had.

After dinner, we headed out to the backyard and sat around the firepit. I knew this was why I had been brought here in the first place, so when we all settled in, I shared my story—how I'd come to know Jesus, the ways He'd been faithful to me, and how He'd brought me to the ministry I was doing at the time with Kids Across America.

After I finished my story, I looked around the firepit at everyone and said, "Look. You're all great people, but if I'm being honest, this is the last place I want to be right now. I'm supposed to be in San Diego, having dinner with the friends I was flying out there to see in the first place. But for some reason, when I fell out of the sky today from twelve thousand feet, I landed in your backyard.

"Tomorrow, I'm going to fly this little airplane the rest of the way to San Diego. So I've got a question for you: if there were a 10 percent chance that this airplane would crash between here and San Diego, would you get in it and go with me?" They shook their heads. "What about a 5 percent chance? A 1 percent chance?" They shook their heads again. "No," I said. "No, I wouldn't either. Unless I know with 100 percent certainty that I'm going to land safely, I'm not getting in that airplane and flying it anywhere."

"Look," I said, directing my attention to the captain's wife. "The deal is, we're all going to die. That's just a fact.

Are you willing to take a 10 percent, 5 percent, or even a 1 percent chance that you could be eternally separated from your two precious children, your best friend, and your husband, who's been praying for you constantly for the last two years?" I looked around at the group. "Are you willing to take that chance, that you would spend eternity separated from your loved ones and everything you love about this life on earth?"

The captain's wife and her friend both looked at me and said, "No."

I nodded. "I wouldn't either. Look, your husband and neighbors are praying for you right now, and so am I. It's divine that I'm here tonight. I didn't want to be here, but God brought me here to be with you, and at this moment, there's nowhere else I'd rather be. Is there any reason why you wouldn't pray a little sinner's prayer with me and invite Jesus Christ into your lives tonight?"

And they did. That evening, around a firepit with people who'd been total strangers to me just a few hours earlier, I had the joy of watching two precious ladies commit their lives to Jesus. There were hugs and tears, and it felt like a weight had been lifted that none of us had realized was there.

The next morning, I got up early and went straight to the base with the captain. Charging the airplane battery overnight had done enough for me to get my plane back in the air, and I flew it to a neighboring airport where I hoped I might be able to find a mechanic who could help me make repairs. I arrived at the airport's Flight Based Operation Center, but it was completely unattended—not a single person was around who could help me.

There was a card taped on the door with a phone number, so I called it, and sure enough, the mechanic answered the phone. I explained my situation to him, and he agreed to come and repair my alternator. I told him I'd have the engine compartment uncowled by the time he got there, and that I'd help him remove the alternator when he arrived.

He showed up about half an hour later, and we started digging in. We pulled the alternator apart, which I was still convinced was the problem, and he started examining the brushes. As he did, I got a feeling that I was supposed to talk to this man about more than just my airplane. So, I asked him to tell me about his wife and kids.

"Well, it's a sad story," he said. "My wife left me about six weeks ago. I've made some bad choices, and I haven't been the kind of husband she wants or deserves. I love her so much, and I miss her. But I messed up, and I think it's too late."

"Well," I said, "what if it's not too late? I think right now, your garden is full of weeds. So, you have to figure out what to do about the weeds. When I have weeds in my garden, I pull them or spray them, and when my bushes get overgrown, I prune them. We all need pruning—I need it myself. And it sounds to me like you need a lot of pruning."

He nodded. "Yeah," he said, "you could definitely say that."

I looked him in the eye. "Do you really want her back? Do you really want to save your marriage and be back with your wife and kids?"

"Absolutely," he said. "I'd do anything. I would give anything to be back with them."

"Okay then," I said. "The first thing you need to do is acknowledge you need God's help. You're headed over a cliff, and you need to receive Jesus Christ as your Lord and Savior and allow Him to walk beside you as you seek to bring reconciliation back to your family. Are you willing to do that?"

"I'm willing," he said. "Let's go."

"Okay," I said. "Just pray this little prayer with me." And right there beside the plane, he got down on his knees, and I led him in a prayer to receive Jesus into his life.

"Now," I said, "I want you to go to the nearest flower shop, and I want you to buy every single rose they have. Every single one. I'm going to pay you well for helping me out here, so I don't care how many; I don't care if they're red, yellow, white, blue, whatever—just buy them and have them sent to your wife, or deliver them to her yourself with a short note. In your note, tell her in your own words that you just want her to know that you love her, and that you're sorry for the pain you've caused her. Tell her you've given your life to Jesus, that you want your life to be different from this point forward, and that you want your marriage with her to grow stronger instead of growing apart."

"Done," he said. "I'll do it as soon as we're finished here."

"Great," I said. "And listen—don't make this a one-time deal. At least every week or two, I want you to write her a note. It can be short, and it doesn't have to be fancy—you can even write it on a napkin or the back of a receipt. But just write her a note to let her know that you love her, you're thinking of her, and you're praying for her. It may take some time, but my sense is that she'll come around."

He nodded. "I'll do it," he said.

"And one more thing," I said. "This is important. You need to find a good evangelical church to start going to every Sunday—a place where you can pray, meet with God, and worship with other people who can come alongside you and support you in your faith. When your wife is ready, take her with you too, if she's willing."

"Yes," he replied. "I'll do all of it. Thank you so much."

We prayed together, and after he finished with my plane, I finally got in the air toward San Diego. We stayed in touch, and eventually I learned that it all worked out. Their marriage was restored, and he found a church and got involved just as I'd encouraged him to do.

I was able to make it the rest of the way to San Diego. I met with the dear folks I was scheduled to see in the first place, and we had a great time together. But I'll never forget that trip—not for the parts that went as planned, but the parts that didn't.

I took off from Branson at the start of that trip with a specific plan in mind. And it was a worthwhile plan—I was going to spend time meeting with people who were deeply committed to our ministry at Kids Across America Kamps. But even though I'd planned something good, God had planned something better.

He knew that near El Centro, California, there were three people who needed to hear about Him. And He knew that there'd be a pilot in the sky right above them on a cold night in February who, by His grace, He'd prepared to share a message that could change the course of their eternity.

He knew what He was doing. Just like He always does.

> *Someday you'll hear that Gregg Bettis is dead. Don't believe it! I'll be more alive than I am as I write this, and I'll be already experiencing all of the eternal joys of heaven in the glorious presence of God.*
>
> —Gregg Bettis

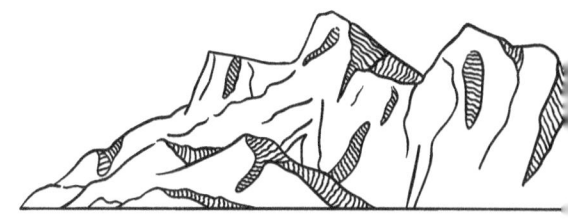

CHAPTER 10

The Crash

ABOUT FOUR MONTHS later, on June 10, 2004, I was flying home after a trip to Tulsa. At around 5:30, I stopped in Branson to top off my fuel tanks. I was ten minutes from my final destination, a small private airstrip near our camps on the shores of Table Rock Lake—one I often used when returning from these trips. I had told my wife when she dropped me off that morning that I would be back on the ground by six, and I was right on schedule.

I hopped back into my plane. A Flight for Life helicopter was also about to take off, and he radioed that he was going to be two thousand feet to the north. I responded that I was going to be fifteen hundred feet to the west. He took off, and then I took off, headed toward Table Rock Airpark.

Nothing seemed out of the ordinary as I navigated toward the small airstrip I had landed on probably a hundred times.

I was ready to get on the ground and see my wife after a long day of meetings and travel. As I flew over the beautiful lake, the weather was a little breezy, but nothing unusual or extreme. I could see the crystal-clear reflections of the sky and clouds reflecting off the lake like a mirror. I could see the runway off in the distance, getting closer. But there was one thing I didn't see.

A mini cyclone spun just low enough over the water near the approach end of the runway that it was out of my line of sight. But it was spinning just high enough to slam into the right side of my airplane.

I was moments from touchdown, ready to settle onto the runway, when I felt the impact of the right quartering tailwind force me hard to the left. If I continued trying to land, I knew I'd crash into the line of tall trees along the left side of the runway. So, I immediately pushed the throttle to full power and on the right rudder in an effort to turn away from the trees, climb back out, and go around to land safely. Unfortunately, I had three factors working against me: a powerful right quartering tailwind and propeller factor pushing me hard to the left, and that line of trees on the left waiting for me. The runway was only thirty feet wide, making my margin for error incredibly small.

At any other airport—one without trees so close down the left side of the runway—it wouldn't have been a problem. But as I felt my plane being pushed hard to the left, I could tell that I was doomed. A few seconds later, my left wingtip caught the top of the second-to-last tree, which caused my plane to turn squarely into the very top of the last tall tree. I watched in terror as my propeller bent like a paper clip, and I dove straight into the ground at 100 miles per hour.

The last thing I remember before crashing to the ground was crying out to God three times, "Oh God, help me. Oh God, help me. Oh God, help me…"

Then, just for a nanosecond, I felt an overwhelming sense of perfect, absolute peace. And in a flash, the Holy Spirit brought to my mind Psalm 91:1: "Whoever dwells in the shelter of the Most High will rest in the shadow of the Almighty."

———

JANELL HAD PLANNED to come with me that day. Earlier that morning, before we got out of her truck, we had prayed together for God's protection on the flight, and at the end of our prayer she said, "Gregg, we're planning to go to Houston tomorrow. Is there any way I could just stay home from this trip? I have a little shopping to do, and it would be nice to get it done today, if you don't need me."

"Yeah, no problem at all," I responded. "You stay home, get whatever you need to get done, and I'll be on the ground at six tonight. You can just come pick me up."

"Great," she said. "I'll see you soon."

She drove me to the airstrip, we hugged, and just like every time I would leave for a flight or adventure, she said, "Please come back to me!" That's how close she was to being in that airplane with me, and I'm grateful every day that God used that little bit of shopping to keep her from flying with me and ultimately to save her life.

Later in the day, a little before six, Janell drove to the airstrip to meet me. She had just washed her truck, so she parked in a neighbor's driveway a little ways down from where I normally parked at the airport so the dust stirred up from our plane wouldn't get her truck dirty. She waited for me, reading an issue of *New Man* magazine I'd just received in the mail (she always seemed to read them before I did).

And then, she heard the crash. She'd heard a plane coming in, and then she heard a huge bang. The sound surprised her, but she immediately thought to herself that there was no way it was me. She knew how many times I'd landed on that airstrip, and she knew that I'd never had any issues at all. Some other pilots used the airstrip to fly experimental aircraft, and she assumed it was one of them.

But then she noticed people running. Lots of people, from houses all around, coming out their doors, carrying fire extinguishers, sprinting toward the airstrip. And Janell got out of the truck.

She began walking toward the crash site. She could see a crowd of people milling around. But then she got close enough to see the airplane on the ground. Its wings were totally crumpled, and its engine was pushed practically into the lap of the pilot. She knew immediately whose airplane it was. And the reality of the situation hit her. People don't survive crashes like this.

Her husband was probably dead.

I don't remember anything after the crash, but Janell later filled me in on what happened next.

The first person to reach my wrecked plane was a woman who had driven in two hours earlier from Memphis, Tennessee, to visit her brother. She just happened to be a trauma nurse. She reached my airplane and jumped up onto it immediately, preparing to help me. Apparently I begged her to get off the airplane because I'd just filled it with fuel, and somehow I was conscious enough to realize that it could explode at any time. But she didn't pause what she was doing for a second.

"I'm going to stabilize your head, neck, and back," she said.

"This airplane could blow up," I said.

"I don't care," she said. "We're getting you out of here."

There were more people around the airplane now—mechanics who worked at the airport wielded fire extinguishers, circling around the airplane, cutting wires and anything else that could cause a spark. They detached the battery from the plane, and as this heroic nurse was stabilizing me, they kept the plane safe. If there had been a fire, I would have certainly burned to death. But through their heroic efforts and by God's grace, there was no fire, and after using the jaws of life to cut me from the wreckage, I was taken out of the plane safely.

Once Janell realized I was still alive, she called a few family and friends to alert them of my plane crash and to tell them that, miraculously, I was still alive. Our daughter Kaylene's response was, "Mom, it's *always* a miracle that Dad is alive!"

The volunteer fire department was on the scene within ten minutes, and ten minutes after that, the same Flight for Life helicopter I had communicated with earlier arrived. They got the call that there had been a plane crash, and they turned around immediately. For a lot of this time, Janell told me later, I was screaming at the top of my lungs. But I have no memory of talking to anyone or feeling any pain at all.

They cut off my boots and a lot of my clothes, strapped me into a stretcher, and loaded me into the helicopter. I was a mess. I had broken bones all over my body. I literally had bones sticking out of my skin. But apparently, after I'd been loaded onto the helicopter, I asked the Flight for Life nurse if he could please fix my little toe, because it was caught on the door jamb.

"You've got all of these broken bones, and you're worried about your little toe?" he asked.

"Please," I said. "Just really quickly. It'll only take a second. Fix my little toe!"

"I can't get out," he said. "I'm strapped in, and I can't unstrap and fix your toe. We're getting ready to take off."

"Will you please fix my toe?" I said. "If you'll fix my little toe, I'll give you a hundred dollars."

He looked over at me and sighed.

Three days later, as I lay in my hospital bed, the same Flight for Life nurse walked into my hospital room. "Mr. Bettis," he said, "you owe me a hundred bucks."

I looked up at him. "Why?"

"Because," he said. "I fixed your little toe."

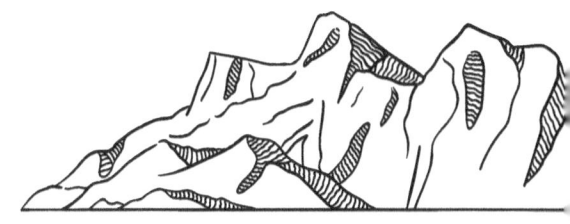

CHAPTER 11

My Seven-Year Knee

> *"I have a great need for Christ; I*
> *have a great Christ for my need!"*
>
> –Charles Spurgeon

I WAS ALIVE. GOD had rescued me from my horrific plane crash. I was lying unconscious in a hospital bed, my body was a mess, and some 90 percent of my bones were broken. But I was alive.

After examining me, the orthopedic surgeon, Dr. Brad Wyrsch, walked out of the ER to talk to my brother-in-law, who had come to the hospital right away. "He's going to survive," the doctor told him. "But his right foot has come completely detached from his ankle, and it needs to be amputated. We're also going to have to take his left leg off above the knee."

My brother-in-law shook his head. "You can't take his leg, doc. Do whatever you need to do—use plates, screws, wires, super glue, whatever it takes. But you have to put him back together."

"I'm sorry," Dr. Wyrsch replied. "Even if I did reattach his foot and cast his knee and leg, he'd be dealing with a significant staph infection. It would be bone-on-bone, the pain would be excruciating, and he'd end up losing his foot and leg eventually anyway."

"I don't care," my brother-in-law pleaded. "Please, do your best to put him back together. He works at a Christian sports camp, and he needs his foot and leg."

The doctor raised his eyebrows. "What camp?"

"Kids Across America Kamps," my brother-in-law answered.

"I just got back from Kanakuk," said Dr. Wyrsch. "I heard Gregg speak. This is *that* Gregg Bettis?"

"Yeah, this is *that* Gregg Bettis," my brother-in-law affirmed. "He's president of Kids Across America, a camp for inner-city kids. You have to somehow save his foot and leg."

"Okay," Dr. Wyrsch agreed, shaking his head. "Okay. We'll put him back together the best we can."

And they did. They worked on me for hours and hours, and in the end, they were able to temporarily reattach both my foot to my ankle and my knee to my tibia plateau. I was alive, and somehow, I was still all in one piece.

But that didn't mean my journey was over. The doctor had managed to put me back together and reattach my ankle and leg joints, but I was still in really bad shape. I was looking at a serious staph infection and the promise of extreme pain.

Despite everything Dr. Wyrsch had done for me, I was at serious risk of losing my ankle and leg anyway if I wasn't able to find specialist orthopedic surgeons who could help me.

As I started the process of meeting with renowned surgeons—the best in the country—things were looking bleak. I met with one surgeon after another, each one distinguished for working with these types of injuries, and the appointments were always the same. They'd take X-rays, put them all up on a screen in front of me, and tell me they didn't see any way to avoid amputation. One after another, these accomplished surgeons told me that I was going to lose my leg and foot.

At the start of this process, I had decided that I'd meet with seven doctors, and if there was no hope, I'd accept that I was going to lose my leg. And after I met with the seventh doctor and heard the same news, I was ready to move forward. Legs are overrated anyway, I thought. I'd get a prosthesis and do what I had to do. I'd adjust, and I'd be fine.

But then, out of the blue, I got a call from my dear longtime friend Jay, who was a prominent plastic surgeon in Dallas. "Gregg," he began, "I know you've met with several great doctors about your leg, but there's one more guy I want you to go see before you let them take it."

I sighed. "Jay, I've seen the best. I have seven sets of X-rays, and every doctor has said exactly the same thing. *Exactly* the same thing."

"I don't care," Jay insisted. "I've got a guy that just might be able to save your leg. He's the best in the world—he takes care of soldiers coming back from Iraq with injuries you couldn't imagine, and he uses a new method that most other doctors won't even attempt. He's in Atlanta. It'll be well worth whatever it costs, I promise—just say you'll go see him."

"Alright," I conceded. "Thanks, Jay. I don't know if it'll be any different, but I'll go see him."

So, Janell and I flew to Atlanta and met Dr. George Cierny. He did the same thing every other doctor before him had done—took a full set of X-rays, put all the pictures on a big white screen in front of us, and then looked at the pictures with us in the room. I knew what was coming next, because it had happened seven times already. He was going to look at the X-rays for a couple of minutes, then look at me, and tell me how sorry he was that he didn't see any way to save my leg.

But after he put the X-rays up on the screen, he stared and stared at them. He studied them silently, looking harder and longer at them than any of the other doctors had. I didn't know what he could possibly be looking at that all the others had missed. But then he turned to me, confident as can be, and asserted, "I can fix you."

I was stunned. "What?"

"I can fix you," he claimed. "And I can do it in one of two ways. I can fix you permanently. But you're going to be non-weight-bearing for eighteen months."

"You're kidding," I said. This wasn't what I wanted to hear.

"No," he stated. "Not kidding. We'd cut off the bottom third of your femur and the top third of your tibia and fibula, and we'd put in titanium rods and a cadaver knee of a twenty-year-old. Once your knee has recovered, it will be stronger than it's ever been.

"But it's going to be extensive. It's going to take time to heal, and if you're not willing to do that, then I'm not going to do that surgery. I've done it on high-level athletes in almost every major sport. The ones who've stayed off their leg as long as I asked them to have had success, but the ones who thought they were strong enough and tried to come back early didn't. If we go this route, you'll have to do exactly what I tell you to do."

I was flooded with a mix of emotions. I was thrilled that he might be able to fix my leg, but I couldn't imagine staying off it for eighteen months. "Tell me the other option," I pleaded.

"The other option fixes you for seven years, max," he replied. "Maybe only six. Then we're going to be right back here, and we're going to have to do the permanent fix."

"Okay," I said. "What does that look like?"

"Well, we're going to put three external fixators on you. It's called an Ilizarov, and you're going to have about twenty pins and wires going through your knee from the top of your knee to the bottom of your tibia plateau. It's not a permanent solution—there's already too much damage from your crash and the infection."

"But it'll be good for six or seven years?" I asked.

"Yep," he said. "And you'll be walking within a week. But you'll probably wind up in the hospital as many as a dozen times over the next several months because of pin site infections."

I'd heard everything I needed to hear. "That's what I want to do," I responded. "I need to be walking as soon as I can. And maybe it'll last longer than seven years. Maybe God will heal it."

Dr. Cierny shook his head. "God will not heal it," he countered. "You'll be right back here within seven years, and we'll be planning to do the other surgery. You need to understand what you're signing up for if you go this route."

I looked at Janell. "I know it's not permanent," I said. "But I think it's what I need to do. I can't be out of commission for all that time."

Janell agreed. And so, that's what we did. Dr. Cierny performed the surgery that would get me back on my feet in a week, and even though I knew he said I'd be back in seven years, I still hoped that God would heal my knee.

The surgery made me look like a science experiment. I ended up with twenty-one pins and rods going through my knee. I had to wear an Ilizarov apparatus, which was made of three metal rings that went around my leg. Janell's mother kindly altered a few pairs of jeans and one pair of dress pants so that they fit around my knee, so my apparatus didn't show at all unless I was wearing shorts.

But I wore shorts a lot. And to be honest, I didn't care. I was determined to take good care of my knee, but I was also determined not to let it slow me down. I flew to Israel with the apparatus on my knee. I went hiking, flew airplanes, rode horses and camels, and did lots of things that people wearing an Ilizarov apparatus definitely shouldn't have been doing, much to Dr. Cierny's chagrin (I usually didn't ask his permission!).

I did everything I could to take good care of my knee. Whenever I traveled, even internationally, I always brought Epsom salt with me and made sure the home or hotel I was staying in had a good bathtub so I could scrub my pin sites twice a day, every single day. And when I returned to see Dr. Cierny, he told me he couldn't believe what he was seeing.

"I've done thousands of these surgeries over the years," he told me. "You're the first person who's ever come back to me at this point without a single infection. I've never seen it before."

He removed the Ilizarov apparatus, and I felt great. No infections. Back on my feet. I was ready to conquer the world. "Doc, you've done an awesome job," I stated. "I think this thing is healed. I think I'm good."

He shook his head, just like he had before. "I'm glad you're feeling good, Gregg," he responded. "But you need to be realistic. It's great that you've had no infections, but this surgery isn't meant to be permanent. You'll be back here within seven years, and we'll be doing another surgery—the permanent fix."

Well, the seven years went by, and I was still walking, hiking, flying, riding bicycles, doing all the things I wanted to do. I did everything I could do to take good care of it, and I had zero pain, zero infections, zero issues of any kind. I checked in with Dr. Cierny regularly, and once he even took X-rays. "I don't know how you're still doing it, Gregg," he marveled. "You're still walking on this thing. I've never seen it before."

"Doc, I'm good," I said. "Truly. Zero pain. I really do feel great."

He shook his head. "I'm glad to hear it," he said. "I just don't know how it's happening."

Year eight went by. And then year nine. But then, one day in 2013, I got a call from Dr. Cierny. "Gregg," he said. "There's something I need to tell you. I've been diagnosed with pancreatic cancer. I've got about nine months to live. I know you're feeling good about your knee, but if you're ever going to get the surgery, it has to be now."

I was hit with such a mix of emotions. Grief for this man who had given so much to me. Shock to be given such sad, startling news. Anxiety at the thought of suddenly having this surgery that would take me off my feet for eighteen months. I told Dr. Cierny how sorry I was to hear this horrible news. But I knew I couldn't do the surgery.

"Gregg," he said. "We need to get you on the schedule. You've got to get down here so I can take care of your knee, because soon it'll be too late."

"Alright, doc," I said. "I'll come down to see you. But I'm not coming for the surgery. I'm coming to see you, and I'm coming to pray."

I was able to come down and see him shortly after we spoke on the phone, and it was my great joy to see him give his life to Christ. Dr. George Cierny passed away on June 24, 2013, after his battle with pancreatic cancer. He passed away as my brother in Christ, and I can't wait to see him again someday in heaven to thank him again for everything he did for me.

As for my knee? As I write this book, I'm nearing the twenty-year anniversary of my plane crash. Dr. Cierny told me his surgery would last me seven years, and I've made it nineteen (and counting). I still actively participate in extreme adventures that would probably make Dr. Cierny cringe, from flying planes to climbing mountains to going on dangerous 550-mile adventures on jet skis in Alaska. And I've still had no pain and not one single infection.

I believe God healed my knee. And I believe if Dr. Cierny were still here, he'd agree with me. I'm so grateful for what he did for me—for his willingness to save my leg, putting me back on my feet, and giving God the chance to do the rest.

CHAPTER 12

The Grand Teton

> *"Life is not measured by the number of breaths we take, but by the moments that take our breath away."*
>
> –Maya Angelou

THE VERY FIRST time I saw the Grand Teton, I was fifteen years old. I was with my grandmother, and I remember very clearly rounding a corner, seeing the Grand in front of me, pointing at it, and saying, "Someday, I'm going to climb you."

Well, fifteen-year-old me certainly didn't expect that he'd one day be in a plane crash and break 90 percent of the bones in his body, or that his knee would be completely rebuilt, or that he'd have a titanium ankle. Things get a little more complicated as you get older.

After my plane crash, I never imagined that I'd be able to attempt a technical climb again. I didn't even know if I'd be able to walk normally again. But one evening, about fourteen years after my crash, I was having dinner with a dear friend of mine, Dr. Gary Oliver. Gary looked at me from across the table and said, "Gregg, I want to climb the Grand Teton. And I want you to come with me."

Gary didn't have to ask me twice. "I'm in," I said. "Let's do it."

Would my leg be able to handle a technical climb? Would I be strong enough to make it not only all the way up the mountain, but back down as well? I didn't have any way of knowing for sure. But what I knew was that it had now been about twice as long as Dr. Cierny had said my leg would last after the surgery, and I was still feeling great. I still had no pain. And I wasn't about to watch Gary tackle without me the mountain I'd wanted to climb since I was fifteen.

"My friend Kevin is a world-class climber," I told Gary. "He's probably the only guy in the world who'd be willing and able to get a couple of old guys like us up that mountain. I don't know if I'll even be able to make it up with my knee and ankle and everything else. But if anyone can get us to the top, it's Kevin."

I reached out to Kevin, and he agreed, so we set a date. Gary and I spent almost a year training hard to prepare our bodies for the climb. All the while, my family tried to talk me out of it, and they kept it up until the morning they dropped us off at the trailhead to begin our journey. I couldn't blame them. They knew I was an old guy (we planned to reach the summit on my sixty-seventh birthday) with a rebuilt leg, and they didn't want to see anything harmful happen to me. But my mind was set. I was going to do this thing. And so, on July 19, we set off.

It was a two-day climb. On the first day, we'd get to the saddle and camp at that base for the night; then we'd climb to the top the next day. The first tip Kevin gave was for Gary and me to get rid of half the things we had packed to carry with us. He knew we'd need to travel as light as possible, and it wasn't long before I could see why.

On the way to the saddle, we encountered a field full of huge boulders. I shouldered my backpack (which still weighed about forty pounds), and we climbed over one boulder after another. It was a challenging section for anyone to get through, especially two old guys like us. But eventually, we made it through the boulder field, finished the rest of the first day's hike, and made it up to the saddle.

I was okay. I was tired, and I could certainly feel the elevation, but I was healthy, my knee and ankle were holding up, and I hadn't injured myself. We set up camp for the night, and at two o'clock in the morning, we got up to make our way to the summit. The real fun was about to begin.

The path toward the peak was the "technical" part of the climb. It was the steepest part, and it was treacherous at certain points. We had to scale across a two-thousand-foot wall. At one point, we had to climb through an ice tunnel, praying the whole time that it wouldn't cave in on us due to the foot of hail that had fallen the night before we left.

Kevin went ahead of Gary and me the whole way, setting all the anchors and belaying us as we climbed. And the climb wasn't getting any easier.

At one moment, I thought I had reached my limit. I needed to make a move that was particularly challenging, and I didn't think I could do it. I didn't think my body was flexible or strong enough. And so, I prayed, "God, I can't do it. I don't have the strength. I'm done."

And just as clearly as anything Kevin or Gary said to me on that day, I audibly heard God speak back to me: "I've got you. You can do it."

Then I heard Kevin's voice. "Come on, Gregg!" he shouted. "You've got this. You're going to do it. You're going to do it!"

By God's grace, I did. And then Gary did as well. We kept grinding it out together the rest of the way up the mountain, following Kevin one step at a time. Just before noon on my sixty-seventh birthday, we reached the summit.

Right before we reached the top, I remember thinking, "Man, it would be so cool to fly a Super Cub plane up and over this mountain." So I could barely believe my eyes when, just as we reached the summit, I looked up and saw a little yellow Super Cub airplane circling us in the air. The pilot and his wife were inside, and they were so close to us that I could literally see the whites of their eyes. It was as though God wanted to say to me, "See? I hear the desires of your heart. And I care about them." Talk about a great birthday gift.

We ate lunch and hung out on the summit for about thirty minutes. But we knew some bad weather was coming, so before long we packed up and, after eating some energy snacks, began our descent. I knew that the challenge wasn't over—climbing down can be even more technical than climbing up—and we wanted to get down without having to battle the elements any more than necessary.

We made good progress at the start. We'd been able to set up easy repels for the first fourth of our descent. But then we reached a point where our only option was a very technical repel down. Snow had just started falling, which made visibility a challenge. Even worse, we didn't have ropes long enough to get from where we were to the next ledge.

Kevin had a plan, as always. "Gregg," he said. "I'm going to have you go down first. You're going to set the anchors, we'll come down to you, and then I'll belay you both the rest of the way down to a ledge."

And that's what I did. I was able to go down and set the anchors. Our rope was about forty feet short of what we would have needed to make it to the ledge, but Kevin's plan worked without a problem, and we all made it.

It was a difficult descent. We took a short break on the ledge, and then we started again, repelling down a sheer vertical wall.

Snow was falling harder now. I got down about fifty feet from the ledge we had rested on, and so much snow was blowing everywhere that it caused a total whiteout. I couldn't see my own hands or feet. I felt like I was inside a thick cloud. And this lack of visibility wouldn't have been a problem, except that I also couldn't see that just below me was an overhang.

I jumped out and down, but when I landed, there was no place for my feet.

I hit the wall hard. The impact knocked my helmet completely off my head. But my main concern was my arm. As soon as I felt the impact, I knew something wasn't right. My arm was very sore, and it wasn't working quite normally. It wasn't strong. Hanging there repelling off a mountain, I was pretty sure that I had broken it.

I could feel my arm enough to know that it didn't seem bent out of shape, which was good news—it wasn't a compound fracture. I tested my arm to see if I could use it at all. There was pain, and it was weak, but I could move it. It wasn't what I really needed it to be, but I could use it.

I managed to make it down to the next ledge, and then we made our way—a bit more slowly than before due to the weather and my arm—back down to the lower saddle. We packed up our gear, and then we started hiking the rest of the way down, through the boulder field and back to the base of the mountain.

Janell, Kaylene, and her husband Bryan all waited for us at the base of the mountain. I had told them that we'd be back by four o'clock that afternoon. But four o'clock came and went. And then five o'clock came and went. And we still weren't back. Janell is a bit of a worrier—hard to blame her, based on my history—and she started worrying. She asked other climbers coming down if they had seen us, and no one had. She knew there were several different trailheads that led to and from the summit, but that didn't make the wait any easier for her.

The Grand Teton summit—an experience of a lifetime!

As six o'clock approached, she saw two helicopters flying down from the summit of the mountain with baskets cabled underneath them. People were strapped in the baskets, and Janell was certain that I was one of them—that I hadn't made it, and they were flying me back to a hospital right then. She found a park ranger and asked who was in the helicopter basket, but they didn't have anything helpful to tell her.

Finally, at around 6:45—almost three hours after I'd told her we'd be back—she saw us. I could tell she'd been crying, and I felt terrible. But I could also tell she was grateful to see me in one piece. I hugged her, and then my daughter and son-in-law, and then I looked up at the mountain I had just climbed.

God has done a lot of big things in my life. But I never would have dreamed that I'd be able to complete a climb like this after my plane crash. He pulled me out of the wreckage of that plane, preserved my life even after I'd broken some 90 percent of the bones in my body, and healed my leg even after seven of the top surgeons in the country said there was nothing that could be done. But even after all of that, the thought of doing what I'd just done—conquering the Grand Teton—would never have seemed remotely possible.

Our God specializes in impossible things. This climb was one of the most meaningful experiences of my life, not just because it was some great personal accomplishment, but because I experienced God's kindness, goodness, and faithfulness firsthand in a way I never had before. He healed me, He preserved me, He protected me, and He was with me the entire way up and down that mountain.

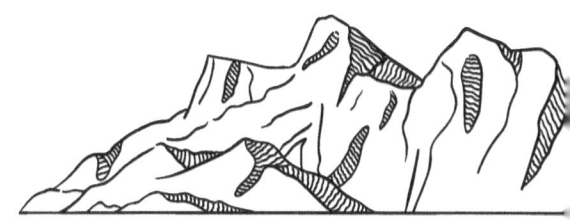

CHAPTER 13

Piranhas, Hippos, and Gorillas

> *"To belong to Jesus is to embrace*
> *the nations with Him."*
>
> –JOHN PIPER

G OD HAS HELPED me conquer all kinds of mountains in my life. And not all of them have required climbing gear.

Just before my daughter Kaylene graduated from Westmont College, I got a call from a friend of mine named Kathy Wills, who had connections with the White House. George W. Bush was president at the time, and Kathy told me Laura Bush was looking for someone who could come alongside her and assist with her communications, particularly in the traveling she did as first lady. Kaylene's degree was in communications, and Kathy wondered if she'd be interested.

I checked with Kaylene, and she was interested—she told me if God could use her in the White House, that would be awesome. So, I called Kathy back, but when she answered, she explained, "Gregg, I've got good news and bad news. The bad news is that Laura decided to hire someone internally for the position I asked you about."

My heart sank a little. "Okay," I said. "What's the good news?"

"Well," she said, "the good news is that George needs somebody. Do you think Kaylene would still be interested?"

So, Kaylene went to work in the White House after all, moving to D.C. right after graduation and supporting President Bush by interviewing and scheduling people who wanted to meet with him. She had always sort of wanted to be the next Barbara Walters, and while in this position she actually got to meet and speak with Barbara Walters.

A regal experience with Janell, Kaylene, her husband Bryan (behind the camera), and our granddaughter Amy Grace.

At the end of President Bush's last term, Kaylene was offered a job as Administrative Assistant to Doug Coe, the founder and leader of the National Prayer Breakfast. She often got to listen in on his meetings with political leaders from countries all over the world. She even had the opportunity to travel to East Africa to visit missionaries who were supported by the International Foundation and who led ministries to young people in Ethiopia, Uganda, and Kenya. After she returned from her trip to Africa, she came to see me.

"Dad," she shared, "I met kids there who were orphans, many of them begging on the side of the streets. They've been through trials and suffering I can't even imagine." She looked at me with puddles in her eyes. "You've got to go and do something to help them."

"Kaylene, that's awful," I sympathised. "But I can't go. Not right now. I've got way too much going on here, and there's no way I could get away."

"There has to be some way you could go help, Dad," she pleaded. "They need someone, and I know that you could help them."

I didn't know what to say. "I'm not sure if there's any way I can help, Kaylene," I replied. "But I'll think and pray about it. I can tell how much you care about those kids."

I felt for Kaylene, and even more for the kids. It wasn't that I didn't want to help. But I was ten years into my role as president of Kids Across America Kamps, and I couldn't just leave to start a camp in Africa. It wasn't that simple. I had too many commitments to break away from.

Not long after my conversation with Kaylene, I got a call from my legendary dear friend Tom Ritchey, who was inducted into the National Bicycling Hall of Fame as the grandfather of mountain biking in California. He had just come back from a trip to—where else—Rwanda, where he was working to start an Olympic cycling team. "Gregg," he urged. "You've got to go help these kids. You wouldn't believe what it's like over there."

"Have you been talking to Kaylene, Tom?" I asked.

"What? No, I haven't," he said. "Why?"

"Well, she just told me the exact same thing. I'm trying to understand why you two want me to go to Africa." I paused for a moment. The truth was, I knew this probably wasn't a coincidence. "Look, Tom, here's the deal. I'm not making any promises, but if this is going to happen, I'll need you to help set up a few meetings for me first. I want to meet with the top religious leaders, top political leaders, and anyone else who might impact what we can do there. Then I want to see the top five properties that we might be able to build a camp on. If you can help arrange those details, I'll go."

It shouldn't have been a surprise to me that all the meetings I requested were set up without a hitch. I honestly didn't want to go to Rwanda. It wasn't that I didn't care about the kids—my heart hurt for them and everything they'd been through. But I had significant camp responsibilities here in America. I didn't have time to be traveling halfway across the world to set up a brand-new camp in a country I barely knew anything about.

But Tom had come through on his end of the bargain. I didn't really have any excuses left. So, with the generous support and blessing of my board at Kids Across America, I hopped on a plane to Rwanda.

From left to right: Me, Tom Ritchey, Martha Ritchey (Tom's wife), and Peb Jackson.

I was able to meet with all the leaders I had requested, and the feasibility meetings and study went better than I could have hoped. Everyone was very enthusiastic and supportive of the idea of opening a camp for these kids, and they had lined up several potential sites for me to visit to consider as we were preparing to build it. The Rwandan President Kagame himself was so excited about the idea that he wanted us to build the camp on his own property, and he invited us to go and visit it first.

President Kagame and I shared a mutual friend, and the friend led us as we made our way to tour the president's property. When we arrived, I was struck by just how beautiful it was. I had specified that any land we considered for the camp had to be on a waterfront so we could have access to water for camp activities, and the president's land looked perfect.

"It's absolutely beautiful," I told my friend. "I really love it. But we want to be respectful of the president's property. If we set up the camp here, would we be able to set up a beach waterfront for swimming and boating?"

"Swim? Oh no, they can't swim here," my friend replied.

I was confused. "Why is that?"

"Because of the piranhas, of course," he replied.

I almost laughed. Good thing I asked! "You're right—we certainly don't want these kids swimming with piranhas." I turned to the folks who were guiding me through this process. "It's really important that we find a camp property that's going to be safe for the kids. Maybe we should go and check out the next option?"

So, we did. They took us to a beautiful safari game park and resort where we all stayed for the night, and the next day we drove out to a site on the shores of another scenic lake. It looked great—I could see it had potential for a waterfront that would be perfect for what we needed, and the property itself was incredible. I was already starting to imagine how it might come together as I reached to open the door of the Jeep to hop out and have a look around.

"Stop!" one of the guides cried out. "Don't get out of the Jeep."

I sat back in my seat. "Why?" I asked. "What's going on?"

"There's a baby hippopotamus down by the water," he said, pointing. "And his mama's up there in the trees. Trust me—we don't want to be between them."

I shook my head. "Folks," I expressed, "this land is beautiful, but we can't build a camp for kids in a place where the animals might hurt us or kill us. I think we should move on to the next property—one that's going to be safe."

So, we moved on. They took me to Lake Kivu, a gorgeous freshwater lake, and showed me a resort that had been abandoned during the genocide. It was a bit run down, but it was a great start, something we could easily refurbish to meet our needs. And the waterfront seemed perfect—Lake Kivu was a huge lake that would be a great fit for boating and the other activities we wanted to do.

"It looks amazing," I said. "So, are we good for kids to boat and swim in the lake here?"

"Yes!" they said. "Probably."

I raised my eyebrows. "What do you mean 'probably'?"

"Well, there are no piranhas," they explained. "But we have had fishermen who have died as a result of the methane coming up out of the lake."

I shook my head. I felt like a broken record at this point. "We can't bring kids into a place where they might be in danger," I responded. "If this is going to work, it has to be somewhere the kids will be safe, whether they're on land or in the water. Is there another place for us to look at?"

"Yes," they answered. "We have one more—a beautiful property up in Ruhengeri."

"And is there anything dangerous there that's going to harm us, try to eat us, or kill us?" I asked.

"No," they said. "It's completely safe."

I was hesitant to take their word for it, but we traveled to the next site, and it was even more stunning than any of the other properties we had seen. But I wasn't sold just yet.

"It's beautiful," I said. "But are you sure it's safe? The water looks clear—is it usable? Are you absolutely certain this will be a safe and secure environment for our campers and guests?"

"Yes," one of the guides said. "It is completely safe."

"Okay," I said, "any animals that we need to be aware of?"

"Nothing dangerous," they said. "There are silverback gorillas about twenty miles up the road, but they've never wandered down this far."

"That's fine," I replied. "It's great, actually. Donors will love to be able to go see the gorillas when they come to visit the camp."

I wondered why they hadn't just brought me here first. "What's the catch? What's going to be our obstacle here?" I asked.

"Two things," they said. "First, with the condition of the roads here, it's going to be impossible for you to get a well drilling rig up here to drill a well and provide our campers with water."

"That doesn't bother me," I replied. "We can figure that part out. We'll get wells drilled even if we have to take the rig apart and truck it up here. What else?"

"Well, the property is wonderful," they explained. "But it's owned by about ninety squatters, and you're going to have to buy all of them out before you can build anything. But John Rucyahana, the bishop of Rwanda, will help us negotiate with them."

"Okay," I said. "I think this might actually work. Let's see what we can figure out with these squatters, but I think we might have found our winner here."

We spent a lot of time negotiating with the squatters, but we were finally able to purchase the property, and it turned out to be perfect for the camp. I was given 20 percent of my time for two years by my board to commit to the project, but I wound up giving three years. We contracted with Christian Engineers International to help with design and plans, and I hired a country director and president to oversee the project. From the beginning, my ultimate goal was for the camp to be run indigenously, and after a couple of years we turned it over to the Episcopalian diocese of Rwanda, who had the relationships and ability to take the project over and operate it.

Rwanda is blessed with an amazing president, a man who had made the statement that he wanted to see Rwanda become a "purpose-driven nation." They also had an Episcopalian bishop who had an amazing heart for Jesus, young people, evangelism, and discipleship. Although those three years were some of the most difficult years of my life, God showed up in many tangible ways. Countless lives are still being blessed in dramatic ways as a result of the time and energy I spent coming alongside the leadership of that beautiful country.

We laid the groundwork for launching the camp nearly twenty years ago. In addition to completing a feasibility study, developing a master plan, securing the property, and hiring a country director and president, we were able to drill two wells, providing the people of the region access to clean water for the first time. And every time I went over, I was thrilled to hug tons of kids and know one day they would have experiences they'd never even dreamed about, all while hearing about Jesus and how much He loved them.

Initially, I was not excited about going to Rwanda. But just like so many other times in my life, God had plans that didn't line up with mine. And just like every single one of those times, His plans were better. He used Kaylene and Tom to influence me and lead me where He wanted me. And by His grace, He provided a way for me to be there. He worked through our team to help launch something that has impacted the lives of countless precious kids in ways we'll never even know about.

In all my travels, I've never seen hope for our world's young people so desperately needed and yet so whole and bright as I have in Rwanda.

"When we give to others, we receive great joy in return... Make helping those who are less fortunate a priority in your life. Loving others is a catalyst for personal growth and a pathway to purpose and joy."

–TOM COLE

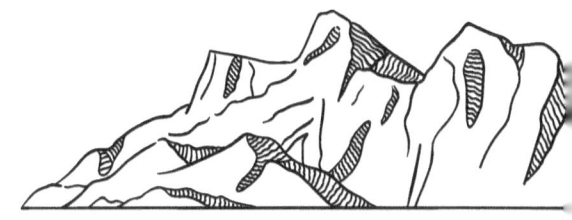

CHAPTER 14

Kids Across America

O VER THE YEARS, we saw God move in incredible ways at Kids Across America. Even before I started working there, God was showing me His plan, and He continued to do so in the following decades.

Way back in the early eighties when Janell and I first lived in Denver, I was directing the Campus Life ministry for Denver Area Youth for Christ. One day after a staff meeting, our director of urban ministry, Luis Villarreal, approached me and stuck his finger in my chest.

"Hey Gregg," he said, "just because you've worked with lily-white rich kids all your life doesn't mean that God's never going to use you to reach the most under-privileged, under-served, and under-resourced—the least of these in our nation."

I stared at him, confused. "Why are you telling me this?" I asked.

"I just want you to know that I believe one day God is going to use you to reach urban youth. These kids need the message of Jesus, and I believe one day in the future, you're going to help bring it to them."

"Man, I'd be a complete duck out of water," I said. "I don't have any experience. What would they think about this white guy with no urban ministry history coming in and trying to relate to them? What could I possibly have to offer?"

That conversation stuck with me. And it came right back to my mind when Joe White called and asked me to come lead Kids Across America Kamps and help reach inner-city youth who needed to hear about Jesus. But I still felt the same way: I knew I had experience leading camp ministries, but I didn't feel I had anything to offer these seasoned urban leaders or their inner-city young people.

I gave Joe the names of some truly great people—African American leaders whom I knew from Youth for Christ, amazing men whom I'd encouraged, led, traveled with, and served alongside. I told Joe any one of them would have been an amazing choice. But Joe and the board had their minds set. They wanted me for this role. And eventually, it became increasingly clear that KAA was where God wanted me too.

That doesn't mean it was easy. I was still a middle-aged white guy coming in to lead a ministry with experienced, world-class leaders of color that was focused mostly on reaching out with Christ's love to African American youth and their mentors. On top of that, KAA had been through some challenging leadership changes in the years before I arrived—they'd had a few presidents come and go in a relatively short period of time.

But as I saw more of the challenges that their ministry was facing, I began to understand all that I could bring to the table, with my passion for relational stewardship ministry and fundraising, as well as my history with camp administration and youth leadership. I didn't have a lot of experience or understanding of working with the culture of the kids who would be coming to our camps. But I did have a lot of experience leading camp ministries and helping to recruit and place leaders in positions to succeed. And from the very beginning, I could see that there were going to be some difficult changes needing to be made if KAA were going to live up to its potential and be a thriving movement that would continue to impact young people in the years and decades to come.

Once I officially accepted the position, I met individually with each member of our board of directors. I wanted to give them a chance to meet me and ask me questions one-on-one before we interacted in an official board setting, and I wanted each of them to know that their input truly mattered to me.

Shortly after several wonderful visits, I attended my very first board meeting. I shared my philosophy and rationale for camp ministry, and I laid out what I felt they needed to know about me, how I was planning to interact with them, and what changes I thought needed to happen very soon.

"The first thing I want to make clear is that we need to tighten up the way we handle our finances," I asserted. "We're currently a million dollars in debt, and I've already begun working on a plan to meet budget and be out of debt within the next twelve months. In addition, our goal will be to have a million dollars in the bank two years from now for emergency and contingency needs we may encounter in the future.

"We also must make some changes regarding the makeup of our board by bringing in both female leaders and leaders of color to reflect the makeup of our campers and their mentors. Having more diversity will challenge us to more fully understand not only the felt needs of our constituents, but the real needs as we seek to make wise decisions for the future.

"But most importantly, I will deeply appreciate our board's support and engagement. I have every confidence that you will roll up your sleeves and make these hard choices along with me. It's important to me that decisions made by our board are not passed based on a majority vote, but rather by a unanimous vote of confidence, especially before moving forward on any major projects that will help us to fulfill our vision and mission. Our God is not a God of confusion, and He will not tell any of us one thing but others something else regarding important decisions. Therefore, I will always encourage our board to pray for and hope to have a unanimous vote before moving forward on matters."

I knew I was asking a lot of the board, especially as someone just starting. Providentially for me, as time would prove, I had the most incredible, caring, and loving board of directors on the face of the planet. I would put them up against any board of directors anywhere, past or present. They were committed, wise, and passionate about the vision and mission of our ministries. And there were no egos present—only people who wanted to give their very best to help KAA become its very best.

Near the end of our first board meeting, Jack Herschend (cofounder of Silver Dollar City in Branson) looked around the table. He had listened hard throughout the meeting, and he'd hardly spoken a word up to this point. "I'd like to make a motion," Jack said, "that we give Gregg everything he asks for during these next two years. He needs to be able to get his vision off the ground, and he needs our unanimous support. I say we give it to him." And every single board member agreed.

Having the board's support meant everything to me over the next few years. It enabled me to make changes that were hard, but that I knew would be for the good of our overall ministry and for the good of the group leaders and campers who would be pouring through our camp gates and seeing their camp dreams come true. Our board's gracious support made it possible for our leadership and teams to accomplish several monumental goals in those first few years, even amid some significant unforeseen adversity.

I sought to stay completely out of the ministry in terms of the day-to-day, boots-on-the-ground work of running our camps and interacting with the campers. This was new for me—it was the first time I hadn't been directly involved in a ministry I was directing. Thankfully, I had the most amazing staff anyone could possibly have asked for.

When I arrived, I had to focus on funding, developing our vision and mission statements, creating policies and job descriptions, establishing a master plan with measurable goals and objectives, and recruiting a few new senior leadership staff members. At the time, we had seven full-time employees, and that number grew to some fifty leadership and support staff during the years I was blessed to serve as president. I could see right out of the chute that funding, recruiting, and lovingly supervising our leadership team were going to be my highest priorities.

So many of the kids who were coming to our camps were desperate to find hope and purpose. Some may have been to church, but they didn't know Christ until they were given a "bubble bath in Jesus" by our KAA leadership, experiencing for themselves the wonder of being loved and cleansed by Jesus. The vast majority of the campers came from very difficult backgrounds, and traveling to this camp out in the middle of nowhere wasn't easy for them. Many of them had never been outside a ten-block radius of their homes.

But when they arrived at KAA, these kids experienced love like they never had before. Our staff showed such grace, patience, and compassion for these kids that the majority of the kids could hardly believe it. If a kid acted out and was told to do fifty push-ups, the counselor would get down and do fifty push-ups right alongside them. And when the camper asked why, the counselor would reply, "Because that's what Christ would have done. Because He loves us, Jesus suffered and died for me, and that's what He did for you too."

In the middle of each week at camp, we had an event we called Cross Talk where our staff would reenact the death and resurrection of Jesus. It was incredibly impactful, and I was always amazed to see how the campers responded. We saw dozens of kids come to Christ at the end of our Cross Talks at each camp every week. After experiencing the love of Jesus firsthand since the moment they arrived at camp, the kids were met by the message of Jesus, and by the end of the week, they didn't want to leave. It was such a privilege to watch up close as these kids' hearts and lives were changed for eternity and they walked away with new hope in Jesus.

When the campers traveled to KAA, they didn't come alone. None of them probably would have made it to us in the first place if it weren't for their group leaders—local urban ministry leaders who had been investing in ministry with the kids all year long. These loving and caring individuals gave up a week of their lives so their group could have this experience.

But it wasn't exactly a luxurious week for these leaders. They stayed in small cabins with bunk beds that were not the comfiest. When they went to worship, they were crammed into a tiny chapel that, at times, was too small for all of them to even be able to sit down.

The problem of inadequate space was getting more pronounced over time—as years went by and our number of campers grew, it became harder and harder for us to accommodate the growing number of group leaders who came with them.

Then I had the opportunity to visit with Tracey Stewart. Her husband, legendary golf professional Payne Stewart, had just passed away, and I traveled to Pebble Beach, California, for his memorial service. Tracey shared with me on the afternoon of Payne's 21-Tee Salute Memorial Celebration that she and her children, Chelsea and Aaron, wanted to do something special in Payne's honor for Kids Across America.

"Gregg," Tracey said, "Payne loved Kids Across America. He would have wanted us to continue to contribute to whatever dream project that's on your horizon."

I knew right away what I wanted to do. We desperately needed to build a purposeful leadership training center and chapel that we could use to bless and support our urban group leaders while they were with us at camp. I deeply desired for them to have a place where they could be comfortable while worshiping together, a place where we could train them to go back home more fired up about their faith than ever. In addition, this center would help us fulfill our vision of "transforming urban youth to impact their communities for Christ," and our mission of "building dynamic Christian leaders by encouraging, equipping, and empowering them through camping and education." I knew these leaders constantly gave so much of themselves to take care of these kids. We needed to be able to take care of them too.

When I went to the board with plans and a proposal that we build a $750,000 leadership training center and chapel, let's just say they were not immediately convinced. "You want to spend three-quarters of a million dollars on a building that you're going to use three months out of the year?" one person asked.

"No," I said, "My plan is to one day use it year-round for weekend retreats. We're going to use it for our group leaders during the summer as well as to provide comfortable lodging for our contributors. In addition, it's going to have an inviting pool with a big deck for lounging and parties, as well as a beautiful driving range—great activities for both our group leaders and our contributors where they can enjoy swimming, hit balls at the driving range, and even receive instruction in a few wholesome activities. The Payne Stewart Memorial Leadership Training Center will reflect Payne's love for God and for kids, and it will honor his family who have been dear friends and extremely supportive of KAA."

I might have sounded a little bit crazy, but I truly believed it was what we needed. And after I fully explained the project, most of the board was willing to support me on it. I remember taking Joe White out for a drive through the woods and all around the area where I wanted to build the training center. As we drove, I talked him through my vision, painting the picture for him of the impact this project could have. "It's going to be a double-ended driving range," I told him. "Forty tee boxes on each end. We'll even have a nice store with camp merchandise appealing to everyone. And the training center itself is going to be fifteen thousand square feet with a big multi-purpose room that we can use for worship or close off for breakout sessions."

"You're really going to do this?" Joe asked me. "You really think this is what we need?"

"We're going to build it," I affirmed. "There's not a doubt in my mind."

"Well," he said, "I'm in. If you believe in this, I'll vote with you."

Joe has always taken time out of his busy schedule to meet with me and encourage me, and he's always been supportive in whatever I felt led to do, whether it was building a leadership training center or traveling to start a camp in Rwanda. But Sam, another one of our board members, was an amazing business and finance guru, and he wasn't always as easy to convince on my out-of-the-box ideas.

"Gregg, I'm sorry," he told me after I shared my vision with the board. "I would like to support you. But the numbers just don't add up."

"Sam, I'd like you to come with me during our lunch break," I requested. "I want to show you what we're working toward. I want you to see the potential this plan truly has before you make your decision."

I took him out to the grounds and showed him around the property a bit, explaining everything to him just like I had to Joe. Then I took him over to a new camp that we were building and walked with him out to the deck of the dining hall, which overlooked Table Rock Lake and a beautiful new pool that had just been finished, but was still empty. "Sam," I said, "can I just pray with you? I'd like to pray that God would lead us in whatever direction He wants us to go for this training center."

I started praying, standing outside on the deck, when suddenly I became aware that Sam was weeping. I looked up at him. "Sam?" I said. "What's up?"

He pointed down at the new empty pool. "There's a golf ball down there. Down at the bottom of the pool."

I had no idea why or how a golf ball would have ever gotten down there, but I looked. And sure enough, right at the bottom of the pool, there was a single white golf ball. It was like God put it there to speak directly to Sam in that exact moment.

"Do it," Sam said. "I don't care if the numbers don't add up. I believe God is in this, and you've got my vote."

So, we did it. We built the Payne Stewart Memorial Leadership Training Center. Tracey came out for the ribbon cutting and grand opening, along with the governor of Missouri and several media outlets, including the Golf Channel. It brought in publicity for the camp that we never would have had otherwise, and we had immediate interest from contributors to come out and stay in the nice suites they'd heard about. These were contributors who most likely would never have come out to visit us in the middle of nowhere to stay in our cabins, but now they were more than excited to come, tour, and experience hundreds of kids ringing the bell after committing their lives to serving and walking with Jesus.

Everyone was blown away—the staff, the board, and our contributors, who continued to come from very long distances, some even flying in privately. The Payne Stewart Memorial Leadership Training Center put us on the map, not only locally, but nationally. And most importantly to me, our group leaders loved it. The memorial honored them and the hard work they did with these kids during the fifty-one weeks of the year that they weren't with us. We had provided them with a first-class facility where they could be equipped, empowered, and encouraged in the work they were doing with their precious kids. We were able to provide valuable opportunities for them to succeed in fulfilling their call as ministry leaders in a way that made them feel valued.

This is only a snapshot of the many amazing things I've seen God do during my time serving as president of Kids Across America Kamps. I've got a thousand stories of God's faithfulness through the years, and I've become more and more convinced that God called me to Branson for a reason. There hasn't been a single moment since moving from Denver when I didn't feel like I was right in the middle of God's will—exactly where He wanted me to be.

Kids Across America honored Janell and me with this plaque after nearly twenty years of serving together.

Seeing how many lives He's changed through Kids Across America Kamps has been amazing. And getting to be a part of KAA and Kanakuk Ministries along with my family, board, staff, and friends has been the greatest joy of my life.

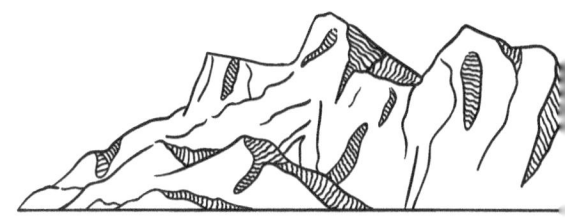

CONCLUSION

> *"There is a river whose streams make glad the city of God, the holy place where the Most High dwells."*
>
> —PSALM 46:4

WHEN I THINK about my life—where I am, where I've been, and where I'm headed next—I imagine myself rafting down a river. I call it the River of No Return. I jumped into it a long time ago, and just like all rivers, the water only flows one direction.

From the very start, God has been the one guiding where I go on this river. He created the river, structuring its contours long before I ever started following Him. I can't always see where I'm headed or what's around the next bend. Sometimes the water is calm and steady; other times I have to paddle through raging rapids.

But in this river, two things have always been true. God is always guiding me. And God is always with me. Every time He's called me outside my comfort zone, His call has led me to more goodness than I could have imagined. He has never left me, never forsaken me, always been with me every step of the way. He has directed my path, guided my steps, preserved my life, and provided everything I've needed, wherever I've gone.

God has guided me to some amazing places in my life. He took me from the wreckage of a horrific plane crash up to the summit of mountains like the Grand Teton and Mount Kilimanjaro. He's allowed me to climb Everest to Base Camp, see glaciers and whales up close in Alaska, and help dear friends launch a cycling team in Rwanda out of the ashes of genocide—a team that made it all the way to the Olympics. He has walked by my side through building camps, leading ministries, raising up leaders, and even writing this book.

If you take one thing from my story, let it be this: when you make yourself available to God, He will use you. He loves you and has a plan for your life, an adventure He's created just for you. And if you offer yourself to Him in obedience, He'll guide you on that path. He'll equip you for the work He's prepared for you to do, and He'll walk beside you every step of the way.

That's my prayer for you: that you will make yourself available to God. With Him, no one is helpless. Ask Him to help you use the gifts and abilities He's given you, and then be obedient to Him. The greatest ability is availability. In my life, in the lives of others I've seen, and all throughout the Bible, one thing is always clear: obedience equals blessing. And wherever God leads you—whatever mountain He's called you to climb—He'll never leave you or forsake you.

Your mountains might look different than mine. But no matter how high the summit seems, if God calls you to it, He will help you climb it.

He'll be with you every step of the way—just like He's always been for me.

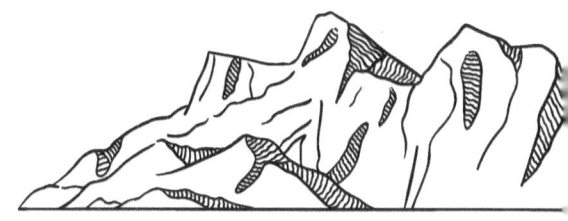

AFTERWORD

by JOE WHITE,
CEO of Kanakuk Ministries &
Founder of Kids Across America Kamps

I N NOVEMBER 1977, a great event occurred on
the shores of Table Rock Lake near the small town of
Golden in southwest Missouri's Ozark Mountains. There
in the scenic junction of the Kings River arm and the White
River arm of this vast and breathtaking lake with 736 miles
of shoreline lies a 183-acre peninsula perfectly suited for
sports camps. For thousands of urban and inner-city kids
from some 435 cities across the United States, this peninsula
is called home because it is here on this sacred ground that
a Christ-filled summer camp called "Kids Across America"
provides a safe and loving harbor where some of America's
most deserving and often forgotten youth find hope, care,
peace, and a freedom that only Jesus can bring.

Kids Across America needed a CEO and courageous leader
in that year, and thankfully a visionary with a can-do spirit

named Gregg Bettis answered the call. Standing on the willing shoulders of his team of able and talented directors—Bruce Morgan, Stephan Moore, Pasha Thornton, Roy "Soup" & Linda Campbell, Eric Williams, Ray & Sylvia Arechiga, Rene Rochester, Ricky Jimmerson, James & Shun Houge, Marlena Gaddison, Dwayne Pano, and soon-to-be-included Dana & Bridget Thomas and Marvin & Angie Daniels—Gregg breathed new life and optimism for growth and depth into that beloved mission.

Over the next twenty years, the camps grew from some 2,400 campers per summer to over 7,000. Adding one camp for older campers and one leadership development camp for the most outstanding high school students marked Gregg's tenure at KAA. With the same passion that motivated Gregg to climb the highest mountain in Africa, standing a foreboding 19,341 feet tall, at age seventy-one and ascending 17,598 to "base camp" of Mt. Everest the year before, Gregg and his team built a life-changing experience for tens of thousands of campers and staff.

Not bad for a man who was told that he might never walk again almost twenty years prior.

Gregg is a delightful person with a smile that could melt a glacier. It is with that captivating and charming spirit that this wonderful book is written.

ACKNOWLEDGMENTS

My heartfelt appreciation to all who have been praying for me, near and far. Your prayers have moved the hands of God in preserving me throughout the course of my adventurous life of living on the edge and experiencing violent crashes and extreme climbs including the mountain within of writing and finishing this book.

Alex Demczak, Will Severns, Annika Bergen, Trevor Waite, and Andrew Blackburn: I am deeply—and I mean DEEPLY—grateful as a first-time author for you and the amazing Streamline team. There would be no book apart from your endless enthusiasm, encouragement, graciousness, creativity, and strategic guidance throughout our journey together in making this book dream come true.

The dynamic staff of Kanakuk Ministries and Kids Across America Kamps—especially Joe White—and our wonderful Woodland Hills Family Church beloved friends: Thank you for providing me with community, the soil out of which this book grew.

Jack & Peter Herschend, Johnny Musso, Shay Robbins, Ted Cunningham, Gary Oliver, Keith Chancey, Tom Ritchey, Kevin Cusack, Ken Davis, Scott Jackson, Steve Rice, Brad Meuli, and the late Ken Atkinson: Without your influence in my life, I never would have written this book. Thanks for your decades of profound friendship. We are brothers for life everlasting.

How do I adequately thank my thoughtful mother and father who brought me into this world, who raised me, and who have always shown their love to me in such tangible ways? Thank you God for my mom and dad. Watching me grow up has no doubt been a fascinating experience, and much of what they read in this book they will have never heard before!

Janell, our beautiful daughter Kaylene, son-in-law Bryan, and adorable granddaughter Amy Grace: Thank you for your support and understanding of the endless weekend and late-night hours and for never complaining about it. I love you!

Sincerely,
Gregg

ABOUT THE AUTHOR

Gregg Bettis, a man full of passion for people and God's kingdom, grew up in Walnut Creek, California, and has been married to his wife, Janell, since 1974. They are the proud parents of their daughter Kaylene and son-in-law Bryan, and grandparents of Amy Grace.

Gregg studied the Old & New Testaments at Ecola Hall Bible School in Cannon Beach, Oregon, in 1972, and the following summer he sensed his call to Christian Camp Ministry while serving at Miracle Ranch Christian Camp near Seattle, Washington. He received his bachelor's in Christian Camping and Recreation Administration with minors in Bible and Christian Education from Biola University. He loved teaching camping courses there and served as a "Mountain Minister" guiding extreme adventure trips with Summit Bound. He studied for a Master of Divinity & Counseling at Talbot and Denver seminaries and became an ordained evangelical minister in 1986 while serving as Elder of Family & Youth at Cherry Creek Presbyterian Church. He served as Denver Area Youth for Christ Campus Life Director for eleven years and in the President's office of Youth for Christ/USA for four years.

Being called to the beautiful Ozark Mountain town of Branson, Missouri, he loved serving as president at Kids Across America Kamps in Branson since 1997 until accepting a kind offer to serve as assistant to the president of Kanakuk Ministries in 2016. Every dream he has ever had has been fulfilled through these two ministries where kids and families continue to come and experience the best summers of their lives!

As an early member of Christian Camping International, Gregg has had the privilege of serving and helping to plant and build camps, reach out with Christ's love to kids, and build dynamic Christian leaders from across America, Canada, and around the world through Christian camping.

He also became an instrument, multi-engine, commercially rated aircraft pilot typed in high-performance turbine jet engine aircraft so he could travel the country efficiently and safely to spend quality time as a "stewardship minister and connector for the kingdom," with caring friends who have tremendous hearts to support far-reaching ministries.

Focused on edifying others, he continues to always be planning the next daring adventure and sharing his deep love for God. His love for Janell, his parents, Kaylene, Bryan, and Amy Grace, along with his zest for life and meaningful connections give him purpose each and every day.